Millennium Perspectives on A.K. RAMANUJAN

Millennium Perspectives on A.K. RAMANUJAN

Edited and with an Introduction by
SURYA NATH PANDEY

ATLANTIC PUBLISHERS AND DISTRIBUTORS

Published by
ATLANTIC PUBLISHERS AND DISTRIBUTORS
B-2, Vishal Enclave, Opp. Rajouri Garden, New Delhi-27
Phones : 5413460, 5429987
e-mail : info@atlantibooks.com

Sales Office
4215/1, Ansari Road, Darya Ganj, New Delhi-110 002
Phones : 3273880, 3285873, 3280451
Fax : 91-11-3285873
web site : www.atlanticbooks.com

ISBN 81-7156-974-9

Typeset at
APD Computer Graphics, Delhi

Printed in India at
Mehra Offset Press, Delhi

PREFACE

The idea of doing a book on A.K. Ramanujan dates back to July 1993 when the poet passed away during a minor surgery in Chicago. Professor Bruce King wrote to me the same year that Ramanujan could not be properly evaluated "because no one had the same range of reading and culture he had" (Appendix-A) and thereby suggested a collective project for the purpose. Incidentally, the editor, *Journal of Indian Writing in English* also found me 'eminently suited to guest-edit' a special number on Ramanujan later that year but I could not oblige him owing to some existing commitments at that time. However, the thought kept stirring me and got an added incentive with the award of a UGC major research project on Indian Poets in English a few years ago. The present volume was planned out to mark the poet's seventieth birth anniversary that fell on 16 March 1999, though it could not keep the deadline. However, I am happy at the fruition of my initial enthusiasm in the form of *Millennium Perspectives on A.K. Ramanujan* for whatever worth it is.

I have been unusually selective in respect of contributors who have written extensively on Modern poetry, Indian, British or American. The volume opens with 'Introduction,' a precise critique of Ramanujan's cultural preoccupations which impart the required scaffolds to comprehend his creative heights. It equips the reader to appreciate the essays that follow with insight and involvement. D. Ramakrishna has ingeniously worked out Ramanujan's poetic creed to demonstrate a pattern between his poetic concepts and practice. I have attempted to correct a critical fallacy in respect of Ramanujan's early poems written in India which need a closer reading and appraisal. Niranjan Mohanty has perceptively identified the poet's 'points of return' to his ancestral connections in a well illustrated essay. Rajalakshmi Gopalan has examined the fusion of the reflective and the introspective in Ramanujan's early verse-volumes to show the nature of these diverse mental practices. Rakesh Desai has explored the ways Ramanujan's poetry engineers the negotiations of art and life. Mohan Ramanan reads the poet's love-pieces to analyse their inbuilt tensions caused by many a determinant including 'unshared childhood.' Much has been talked about Ramanujan's 'split-vision' and Bijay Kumar Das critiques his postcoloniality which enjoined upon him to think of cultures only in reciprocal terms. In an essay marked by perspicacity, E.V. Ramakrishnan locates the poet, a problem of great magnitude and contention. Jayaprakash A. Shinde judiciously traces the centrality of 'family' as the nucleus of the poet's rhetorical devices while Premila Paul focusses on his treatment of human relationship. Shirish V. Chindhade unravels the structural features of some Ramanujan poems to underscore his technical virtuosity. P.K. Kalyani builds up her essay on Ramanujan's posthumous collection *The Black Hen* to examine the quality of his transcontinental experience. The last couple of essays discover the relationship between his poetry and translations. While Rama Nair reads *Speaking of Siva* to reach at a possible link between religious poetry and literary criticism, Rita Kothari deciphers the shreds of cross-fertilisation in Ramanujan's translations (read transcreations) and original poems in English. The annotated bibliography by and on Ramanujan shows the huge bulk of existing scholarship that this versatile poet has invited.

I express my thankfulness to the esteemed contributors who put up with my repeated coaxings and ultimately honoured their commitment. I have benefited from the insightful comments and suggestions of Prof. M.K. Naik and feel beholden to the legendary scholar. I have also incurred a number of more personal debts and to all such friends and students, I am deeply obliged for their advice and observations from time to time.

SURYA NATH PANDEY

CONTENTS

INTRODUCTION

The Axis of Ramanujan's Cultural Preoccupations

A.K. Ramanujan used to self-mockingly describe his position as 'being the hyphen in Indian-American,' a term that unwittingly unfolds the central principle governing his creative universe. In his seminal essay "Parables and Commonplaces," a critique of cultural encounter (a piece incidentally dropped in *The Collected Essay of A.K. Ramanujan,* 1999), Ramanujan identifies E.M. Forster's obsession in *A Passage to India* as 'the complexity of non-communication' which makes the novelist cry, "connect, only connect!" but praises him because he "makes his greatest work out of disconnections" (Ramanujan, 1982 : 147). In a *Second Sight* piece aptly titled "Connect!" the poet almost voices Forster's mania :

> Connect! Connect! cries my disconnecting
> madness, remembering phrases...
>
> Connect
>
> Connect, beasts with monks, slave economies
> and the golden bough. (*CP* : 178)

Multiplicity, whether linguistic, cultural or social seems to have been Ramanujan's *fait accompli* from his very childhood. He has dwelt quite graphically on this aspect of his growing up in his *Daedalus* essay titled "Telling Tales" :

> As we grew up, Sanskrit and English were our father tongues and Tamil and Kannada our mother tongues. The father tongues distanced us from our mothers, from our own childhoods, and from our villages and many of our neighbours in the cowherd colony next door. And the mother tongues united us with them.... Sanskrit stood for the Indian past; English for colonial India and the West.... Each was an other to the others, and it

> became the business of a lifetime for some of us to keep the dialogues and quarrels alive among these three and to make something of them (*CE* : 449-50).

The disarming frankness with which the poet confesses having chalked out his life's mission — "to keep the dialogues and quarrels alive among these three and to make something of them" — manifests his commitment to forge connections between dichotomies. In the process of achieving a synthesis between warring cultural coordinates, this voyager once precisely identified his situation :

> It looks as if I live between things all the time — two (or more) languages, two countries, two disciplines. My translations are a way to keep them all together (Ramanujan, 1995 : 10).

Be it his monumental translations, critical essays or poetic compositions, there is an invisible thread he is looking for, envisaging at times, designing sometimes as well, that lends homogeneity to his marvellous output. Ramanujan's creative odyssey encompasses the ramifications of his struggles to transform his predicament into an artistic virtuosity.

The proper appreciation of Ramanujan's poetry inescapably brings in his marvellous translations both from the angle of his thematic concerns and also of his stylistic preferences. Since he started writing poems in English and translating Kannada and Tamil poems simultaneously in the fifties, it is advantageous to look for his conceptual framework in ancient Indian classics. Coincidentally enough, the publications of his translations and of his original English verse-volumes betray a definite pattern. Each original volume is preceded and followed by a translation in a *samput*-like fashion (to borrow the term from religious vocabulary) : *The Striders* (1966) sandwitched between *Fifteen Poems from a Classical Tamil Anthology* (1965) and *The Interior Landscape* (1967); *Relations* (1971) between *Selected Poems* by G. Sankara Kurup (1969) and *Speaking of Siva* (1973); *Selected Poems* (1976) between *Samskara* by U.R. Ananthamurthy (1976) and *Hymns for the Drowning* (1981); *Second Sight* (1986) between *Poems of Love and War* (1985) and *Folktales from India* (1991). This monotonous statistics shows that with

Ramanujan translation is as central a creative activity as writing of poems in English themselves. To C.D. Narasimhaiah "his translations have struck me as more creative than his own original creations" (Narasimhaiah : Personal Communication). This should, however, not be construed to belittle or denigrate his poetic achievements.

A discourse on Ramanujan's poetic sensibility must profitably begin with clues so subtly enunciated in *Speaking of Siva* which contains "whatever struck me over the past two decades" (Ramanujan, 1973 : 12). This English translation of *Vacanas* in Kannada contains an "Introduction" (lengthiest ever prefaced to any work) which can be justifiably treated as Ramanujan's poetic manifesto, unconscious ramblings of his creative priorities. Moreso because these translations and early English poems had equal claims on the poet's creativity during fifties and also because his verse-volumes contain no prefatory comments. He vehemently affirms, "Translation is choice...a betrayal of what answers to one's needs, one's envies" (Ramanujan, 1973 : 12-13). Undoubtedly Ramanujan's translations help one identify his intellectual and literary needs and also his ambition-out of envy of the past masters — in order to appropriate and repossess the wonderful classical poems" (*CE* : 189).

The most formative influences on Ramanujan, both in terms of perception and expression have been, undoubtedly, the *Vacanakaras,* "great voices of a sweeping movement of protest and reform in Hindu Society" (Ramanujan, 1973 : 12). In fact, the Virasaivism was a movement of social upheaval by and for the poor, the low caste and the outcaste against the rich and the privileged. The Virasaiva saints — unlike exponents of other kinds of Hinduism and like other Bhakti movements in India — do not believe that religion is something one is born with or into. In reality, Virasaivism is a revolt from within while Buddhism and Jainism were revolts from the outside. Ramanujan's "Hindu" poems should be read in the Virsaivite spirit which protests against the aberrations in Hinduism — "Yet we must not forget that this fierce rebellion against petrification was a rebellion only against contemporary Hindu practice..." (Ramanujan, 1973 : 33). He further asserts, "Defiance is not discontinuity.

Alienation from the immediate environment can mean continuity with an older ideal." Ramanujan narrates the circumstances that led to the composition of his "Prayers to Lord Murugan" (*Relations*) which "talks about some Indian attitudes to the Indian past, with which I was somewhat despondently preoccupied at the time" (*CE* : 192). He admits that his is a poem "of lack and self-doubt, in which it is like some other religious poems (*e.g.*, some Virsaiva poems) that I had translated." This must dispel the impression that the poet's critical attitude to Hinduism was an outcome of his exposure to Western ethos. One also recalls that the pieces like "A Hindu to His Body," "Conventions of Despair" and "Still Another View of Grace" are among early Ramanujan poems written in India before his departure to States in 1958. Ramanujan's contemplating conversion to Buddhism at one time shows his affinity with *Vacanakaras* who shared with Buddhists the doctrine of *ahimsa,* non-violence towards all creation.

Bhakti saints, like the Vacanakaras have been called the "great integrators," bringing the high to the low, esoteric paradox to the man in the street, transmuting ancient and abstruse ideas into live contemporary experiences; at the same time, finding everyday symbols for the timeless" (Ramanujan, 1973 : 39). Ramanujan noted this quality of integration even among the Alvar saints, who though differed from Virsaivites in significant ways. In "Afterword" to *Hymns for the Drowning,* he treats their songs as "poetry of connections" :

> This poetry of touching, sharing, seeing, the many in one, is a poetry of connections of continuities. It connects god, gods, and all creation; the god of myth, the god of philosophy, the god in the temple and the god within; speaker, subject, listener; good and evil, hell and even, mythic *then* and poetic *now,* opposites and contraries (Ramanujan, 1981 : 166-67).

Ramanujan's views on culture, Indianness and Western metaphysics are randomly scattered in his other writings also and they provide vital clues to the complex configurations of tensions that sustain his poetic universe. In the essay "Parables and Commonplaces" he dilates graphically, for the first time, on culture and the related issues. He begins with the premise that cultural encounters "lead to definition, redefinition, a dialogue with the other where each returns to himself reflected refracted even alienated and thereby redefined" (Ramanujan, 1982 : 142). He underlines the fact that there is no uniform pattern and degree of cultural interaction as it varies from culture to culture in accordance with its capacity for "coping with, containing, appropriating and domesticating the bizarre, often terrifying alien" (p. 138). He refers to the story of Ramaswami and Madeleinne in Raja Rao's *The Serpent and the Rope* to comment on the quality of cultural assimilation :

> Rama the Brahmin studies Abelard and quotes medieval French. His wife Medeleinne becomes Buddhist, her low bed has a yellow bed-cover with *mandals* and *chakras*. Though they part and the child of their union, Pierre-Krishna, dies, in them East has passed into the West, and the West into the East — with one difference. The Easterner, the brahmin is unchanged; the Frenchwoman utterly changed (Ramanujan, 1982 : 146).

The Easterner Brahmin may remain unchanged but this phenomenon does bring about a qualitative change in his perception and approach. Ramanujan confiding his own experience admits "feeling himself translated a little in each encounter" and learning "a good deal about myself, and about the Indian arts" (p. 140). The most remarkable aspect of this transaction is rather amazing — "the encounters begin with emphasis on differences and end in a moment of communication below the threshold of language — often a recognition of the body's universalities whether it is pregnancy and birth, or a mother's death and a son's mourning, a recognition of oneness, however, momentary" (p. 145).

When it comes to deliberating on the Indian context, Ramanujan underscores its terribly perplexing plurality and also its attendant constraints in his essay "Classics Lost and Found" :

> Indian tradition is not a single street or a one-way street but consists of many connected streets and neighbourhoods... India does not have one past but many pasts (*CE* : 187).

He further observes that like other cultural constructs, the past changes as one attends to it because "In a culture like the Indian, the past does not pass. It keeps on providing paradigms and ironies for the present...." His interpretation of modernity (with echoes of Eliot) has a postcolonial bias about it :

> ...modernity, itself a new attitude to history and tradition, with a new kind of pride in the past, also discovers and includes the Indian past, through new techniques of discovery and through a juxtaposition of "the pastness of the past" and its "presence" (*CE* : 189).

In another essay, "Where Mirrors are Windows" also, Ramanujan, resisting the 'monism' and even 'cultural imperialism' of proponents of a single 'pan-Indian Sanskritic Great Tradition' reiterates :

> ...cultural traditions in India are indissolubly plural and often conflicting.... What we call Brahminism, Bhakti traditions, Buddhism, Jainism, Tantra, tribal traditions and folklore, and lastly, modernity itself, are the most prominent of these systems. They are responses to previous and surrounding traditions; they invert, subvert and convert their neighbours (*CE* : 8).

He traces two organising principles among these systems of culture — context-sensitivity and reflexivity of various sorts — both of which constantly generate new forms out of the old ones. He dives still deeper into their mutual correspondences :

> Where cultures (like the "Indian") are stratified yet interconnected, where the different communities communicate but do not commune, the texts of one stratum tend to reflect on those of another : encompassment, mimicry, criticism and conflict, and other such relations are expressed by such reflexivities (*CE* : 9).

These grammatical items take us to still another essay "Is There an Indian Way of Thinking? — An Informal Essay" where explicating Indian cultural syndrome *vis-a-vis* Western culture, he comments :

> In cultures like India's, the context-sensitive kind of rule is the preferred formulation. While the Western tradition

> is context free based on a premise of universalisation.... In 'traditional' cultures like India where context sensitivity rules and binds, the dream is to be free of context.... Neither the unique nor the universal, the two often contradictory, concerns of Western philosophy, art and polity, are the central concern of the Indian arts and sciences — except in counter-cultures and modern attempts (*CE* : 41-49).

Whether religion or social structure or literary conventions or Indian aesthetics itself, Ramanujan is prone to search for categories within categories. He looks at "'modernisation' in India as a movement from the context sensitive to the context free." In cross-cultural interactions, the two diametrically opposed cultures invariably cross fences. In one of his well-known statements, Ramanujan has singled out the ingredients of culture :

> Just as our biological past lives in the physical body, our social and cultural past lives in the many cultural bodies we inherit — our languages, arts, religions and life-cycle rites (*CE* : 184).

Ramanujan has modelled his poems broadly on Cankam (pronounced Sangam poetry), which he classifies into two kinds — *akam* and *puram*. While *akam* relates to lyrical poetry, *puram* is associated with narrative poetry. *'Akam'* which means inner is confined to subjective poetry while *puram* (meaning outer) is a big umbrella and contains all other types of pieces in its category. To quote him :

> *Akam* poems are love poems; *puram* poems are all other kinds of poems...; it is the "public" poetry of the ancient Tamils, celebrating the ferocity and glory of kings, lamenting the death of heroes, the poverty of poets. Elegies, panegyrics, invectives, poems on wars and tragic events are *puram* poems (Ramanujan, 1967 : 101).

As to the niceties of technique, Ramanujan has drawn heavily on *Vacanakaras* whose style is marked by repetitions ordered towards a crescendo, a climax of denial, as in "Anxiety" (*CP* : 29) or a climax of assertion as in "Love 1 : What she said" (*CP* : 219). The tendency to cycles or sequences of poems so pronounced in Ramanujan's later poetry has its roots in *Vacanas*. In its original version the poem titled "Elements of Composition" comprised fourteen poems *viz.*, "Elements of Composition," "Questions," "Snakes and Ladders," "A Poor Man's Riches 1 and 2," "Aliens," "Drafts," "Middle Age," "The Difference," "Dancers in Hospital," "Connect!," "Looking for the Centre" and "Waterfalls in a Bank" which are now independent pieces. While insertion of sections in a Ramanujan poem is a common pattern in all the volumes, some pieces like "Love" and "Mythology" have sequence pattern in *The Black Hen*. Among tones of speech, chatty talk characterises *Vacanas* and this is a notable feature of Ramanujan's poetry in poems like "The Hindoo : he doesn't hurt a fly or a spider either" (*CP* : 62-63). Among significant similes and analogies borrowed from Virsaivite poetry include 'the seed and the tree,' 'the spider and its self-woven web' and 'the dance and the sport.' The rhetorical endings lead to a state of heightened insight in *Vacanas* and Ramanujan sometimes employs this device when the situation so warrants as in "Birthdays" (*CP* : 206-07). Meditating over the phenomenon called death, the poet muses : "Is it a dispersal/ of gathered energies/back into their elements.../a reworking into other moulds.../and forms clocked into seasons?"

As an artist Ramanujan was open to influences and critical concepts and one comes across repetitions in his critical essays occasioned by his unusual knack of 'constantly energising familiar patterns with unexpected new alignments and rearrangements.' Vinay Dharwadker has very precisely commented on his critical position :

> When he found an intellectual position that sustained all his interests — such as Anglo-American New Criticism in the 1950s. French structuralism, Russian formalism and German critical theory in the 1960s and 1970s, and some aspects of French deconstruction and American and Indian feminism in the 1980s, he used it as vigorously and comprehensively as possible to elucidate many different texts, genres and themes (General Editor's "Preface," *CE* : 9).

However, no critical concept was sacrosanct in itself for him and the moment he spotted the inadequacies of a particular perspective, he was out to review the whole thing afresh, as in the case of the structuralist logic of binary oppositions in the early 1980s which enjoined upon him to approach his material with a new understanding of their values and meanings. It is this encyclopaedic range of exposure and diverse accomplishments which led Ramanujan to confess in the well-known statement :

> English and my disciplines (linguistics, anthropology) give me my "outer" forms — linguistic, metrical, logical and other such ways of shaping experience; and my first thirty years in India, my frequent visits and fieldtrips, my personal and professional preoccupations with Kannada, Tamil, the classics and folklore give me my substance, my "inner forms," images and symbols. They are continuous with each other, and I no longer can tell what comes from where (Parthasarathy : 96).

Ramanujan admired *Vacanakaras* who laid thrust on moving (*jangama*) as opposed to standing (*sthavara*) — "Things standing shall fall/but the moving ever shall stay." (Basavanna, 820, Ramanujan, 1973 : 19) and thereby established the superiority of their quality of worship. Without entering into the minute connotations of the word *Jangama* in religious terms, Ramanujan can be regarded as a *jangama* poet, communicating his 'truth in fragments' to connect people despite inconsistencies and contrasts. Looked at from another angle — "These fragments I have shored against my ruins" (Eliot : 67) — his creative work is an attempt to "set my lands in order." In the last piece of *Collected Poems* titled "Fear No Fall" (one may read fear no fragmentation), the poet derives strength from the story of Tamil Saint Arunagiri that no fall is so deep that one cannot emerge from again. Once the wandering saint found himself "lying in the lap of a very old man" *i.e.,* his god Murugan, his life-style was changed — "leaving Arunagiri a lifetime, of seeking and finding and losing Him again and again..." (*CP* : 276). A poem of spiritual commitment it is a serious introspection on religious experience — to 'seek, to find, to lose' only to seek again and again and thus continue the cycle of human efforts.

The poetry of Ramanujan explores the possibilities of meaning and to that extent it is 'a criticism of life.'

WORKS CITED

Eliot, T.S. 1954. "The Waste Land" in *Selected Poems.* London : Faber.

Narasimhaiah, C.D. A personal communication to the author, dated 24 May, 2000.

Parthasarathy, R. 1976. *Ten Twentieth-Century Indian Poets.* New Delhi : Oxford University Press.

Ramanujan, A.K. 1999. *The Collected Essays of A.K. Ramanujan,* ed. Vinay Dharwadker. New Delhi : Oxford University Press, Referred to as *CE.*

——, 1995. *The Collected Poems of A.K. Ramanujan,* ed. Vinay Dharwadker. New Delhi : Oxford University Press. Referred to as *CP.*

——, 1993. Cited in "Cultural Voyager" (Obituary), *Times of India.* 14 July : 10.

——, 1981. *Hymns for the Drowning.* Princeton : Princeton University Press.

——, 1967. *The Interior Landscape.* Indiana : Indiana Univ. Press.

——, 1982. "Parables ad Commonplaces" in *Writers in East-West Encounter : New Cultural Bearings,* ed. Guy Amirthanayagam. London : Macmillan : 138-49.

——, 1973. *Speaking of Siva.* Harmondsworth : Penguin.

1

Ramanujan's Credo

—D. RAMAKRISHNA

In spite of A.K. Ramanujan's status as an Indian American, he is an author and scholar whose presence is felt on the literary scene in India and the United States simultaneously. He is different from the expatriates like V.S. Naipaul and Salman Rushdie who are rootless but look at India as exotic. Ramanujan's rootedness in Indian culture and involvement with American culture has resulted in his skilful articulation of both the Indian and the Western ideas with ease. As a poet, linguist, folklorist, translator, and literary theorist, he is one of the world's foremost intellectuals. He is unique in bringing together two great cultures, having been at home in both.

Ramanujan's intellectual position was determined by his multiple interests in Anglo-American New Criticism in the 1950s, French Structuralism, Russian Formalism, and German critical theory in the 1960s and 1970s, and some aspects of French Deconstruction and American and Indian Feminism in the 1980s (*CE* : 9). That Ramanujan's critical approach is multidimensional is evident from the fact that in his explication of poems he adopts the formalist literary critical method as well as the contextual concerns of ethnography, history and folklore studies. In his explanations of social codes, he depends on social theory, linguistics, poetics and cross-cultural studies. Ramanujan occupies a unique position in Indian letters in synthesizing his varied concerns as a scholar in Dravidian languages, linguistics, cultures and as a translator of Classical Tamil and medieval Kannada poetry with his superb poetic instinct in English language.

I

An author's preferences, attitudes, and ideals may be explicit in his essays and interviews or implicit in his creative writings. The controversy regarding "intentional fallacy" notwithstanding, the intentions of a writer often help us in making a proper assessment of the man and writer. In *Theory of Literature,* René Wellek and Austin Warren describe "extrinsic" approach as that which looks at literature in relation to society, ideas, and the other arts as well as "intrinsic" approach that is concerned with image, metaphor, technique, etc. One has to take into consideration a writer's *oeuvré* in order to make a proper estimate of his objectives. An attempt has been made in the present paper to study Ramanujan's credo by means of a scrutiny of both the "extrinsic" and the "intrinsic" aspects of his writings.

While in his creative writings Ramanujan gives expression to his personal neurosis and existential predicaments, he strives to arrive at a definition of Indianness in relation to the Western ethos in his essays. The creative and the critical aspects of his genius are not at variance with each other. In fact, they constitute the essence of his credo. Ramanujan succeeds in telling the world what is truly "Oriental" about India in his authoritative treatment of Indology, correcting the Western notions about the subject.

As Wendy Doniger says in her Introduction to *The Collected Essays of A.K. Ramanujan,* before Ramanujan, Indian scholars in the U.S. were merely native informants, but Ramanujan "blazed a great path through the centre of Indological studies." To quote her :

> At a time when the American Indological establishment regarded native Indian scholars merely as sources of information about languages and texts, like the raw fibres that were taken from India to be processed in British mills, but seldom as scholars who might have their own ideas about how to process those texts, Raman taught them all how to weave a theory, a folktale, a poem, a book... (*CE* : 3).

Doniger maintains that the scholarship on ancient India can be comprehended properly only by means of the different paradigms that Ramanujan's work made possible.

Unlike the Postcolonialist scholars, Ramanujan has no political agenda in his articulations of Indian thought. His contempt for politics is well known. In a passing reference to Edward Said, Ramanujan says that the discourse on the Orient has become controversial : "Indology is an invention and gift of Western scholarship, an ambiguous gift according to some" (Said : 8). Like Postcoloniality, Orientalism in the Western discourse had been political in orientation. As an Indologist, Ramanujan has proved superior to the champions of both the discourses, having been more deeply involved than others.

Ramanujan maintains that India is multicultural. As he says in his essay, "Where Mirrors Are Windows : Toward an Anthology of Reflections,"

> I would like to suggest the obvious : that cultural traditions in India are indissolubly plural and often conflicting but are organised through at least two principles, (a) context-sensitivity and (b) reflexivity of various sorts, both of which constantly generate new forms out of the old ones. What we call Brahmanism, *bhakti* traditions, Buddhism, Jainism, *tantra,* tribal traditions and folklore, and lastly modernity itself, are the most prominent of these systems (*CE* : 8).

In addition to his recognition of India's cultural plurality, Ramanujan underlines the "vast variety of Indian literature, oral and written, over the centuries, in hundreds of languages and dialects" (CE : 8). He questions the motto of the official Indian literary academy, the Sahitya Akademi, "Indian literature is one but written in many languages," saying "I, for one, would prefer the plural, 'Indian literatures,' and would wonder if something would remain the same if it is written in several languages, knowing as I do that even in the same language, 'a change of style is a change of subject,' as Wallace Stevens would say" (*CE* : 7).

In "Is there an Indian Way of Thinking? An Informal Essay," Ramanujan says that tradition and modernity, the Eastern and the Western, are like the two lobes of the brain. They can co-exist. This is his answer to the protagonists of Postcoloniality. Ramanujan's own stance is that in the Indian way of thinking, there is both subjectivity and objectivity. He disagrees with those who talk about "lack of logical rigour" in the Indian mind. As Ramanujan says,

> They may be using a different "logic" altogether. Some thinkers believe that such logic is an earlier stage of "cultural evolution" and that Indians have not developed a notion of "data" of "objective facts." Edward Said's *Orientalism* cites many such European stereotypes about the "Third World" (*CE* : 38).

In the words of Edward Said itself,

> ...the imaginative examination of things Oriental was based more or less exclusively upon a sovereign Western consciousness out of whose unchallenged centrality an Oriental world emerged (Said : 8).

Even though Said appears to correct the Western notion of the Oriental, meaning the Eastern, except for a mention of Buddhism, he does not deal with Hinduism or Jainism which constitute the major strands of Indian culture and literature. Ramanujan, in dealing with the essence of the complex Indian culture and literature, goes beyond Said, correcting not only the Western notions but also the limited understanding of Orientalism on the part of Said.

At a time when Indian literature meant Sanskrit, and Sanskrit meant Greek and Latin, Ramanujan arrived in Chicago to join Edward C. Dimock and the other "founding fathers" in enlightening the world about the relevance of Tamil, Kannada, Bengali and the other regional languages (*CE* : 3). In his essay entitled "Where Mirrors are Windows" Ramanujan explains further the term "Indian literatures" :

> Various bodies of literary, religious, *sastric,* or ideological materials, as they come into being at different periods, become part of the vocabulary of Indian literatures, Hindu, Buddhist and Jaina texts, especially legends, stereotypes, beliefs and the commonly known controversies among them... (*CE* : 18).

Referring to the pan-Indian network, a repertoire of types and genres that is trans-regional, Ramanujan says that *bhakti,* tantra and folklore relate to each other and also have Hindu, Buddhist and Jain forms — creating overlaps, intermediate genres and indeed a scale of forms (*CE* : 27). In another essay entitled "Some thoughts on 'Non-Western' Classics," dealing with the multiple existences of Indian classics like Ramayana and Mahabharata in oral and written media, in "classical" and "folk" modes, Ramanujan discounts Western classics like *Iliad* and maintains that only the Bible in its hundreds of translations and myriad uses is comparable to the Indian classics (*CE* : 118).

Ramanujan took pains to highlight the multilingual and multicultural aspects of India (Ramanujan, 1991 : 15). The American anthropologists like Robert Redfield and Milton Singer coined terms like "Great Tradition" (involving the ancient pan-Indian Sanskrit texts) and "Little Tradition" (seen as local, mostly oral, and carried by the illiterate) and stressed the need for "texts" of a culture in preference to "fieldwork." Ramanujan argues that these terms need modification, and asserts,

> Written and hallowed texts are not the only kinds of texts in a culture like India's. Oral traditions of every kind produce texts. "Cultural performances" of every kind, whether they are plays, rituals, or games, contain texts, written and oral. In a sense, every cultural performance is a text in itself (Ibidem : 16, 18).

The relation of folklore to performance has been dealt with by scholars like Alan Lomax, Roger D. Abrahams, Dan Ben-Amos and Dell Hymes (Hymes : 45).

Extensively dealing with the multiplicity of Indian literature, Ramanujan argues that not only written texts but also the oral texts are a part of it. Thus, "Cultural Performance," a "text in itself," is linked with folklore in the various languages of India.

According to Ramanujan, the study of Indian folklore has never been a sharply defined field. Overshadowed by Indology, it has a distinguished intellectual history (Blackburn : 1). In his collection of essays on the Indian folklore entitled *Another Harmony,* he says that folktales in several Indian languages like

Hindi, Telugu, Tamil, and Kannada are part of a complex civilization and they are related to the more immediate social and performance contexts. Ramanujan maintains that Indian culture is "a composite of classical, folk, and popular streams" (Ibidem : 26). Popular Culture, despite the use of oral transmission, depends heavily on mass media, transmitted impersonally through "showbiz" salesmanship. On account of urbanization of the modern India, folklore has undergone change as evident in TV and other electronic media, thus tradition changing into modernity (Ibidem : 27).

In his Note to *The Interior Landscape : Love Poems from a Classical Tamil Anthology,* Ramanujan says : "Anyone translating a poem into a foreign language is, at the same time, trying to *translate* a foreign reader into a native one" (Ramanujan, 1967 : 11). Instead of translating every poem line by line, he renders a poem phrase by phrase, paying special attention to the images and their placement. And he makes explicit typographical approximations to the inner form of the poem. In his "Afterword" to *The Interior Landscape,* the translator says that the *Cankam* poetry is classified by theme into two kinds : poems of *akam* (the "inner part" or the Interior and poems of *puram* (the "outer part" or the Exterior). *Akam* poems are love poems : *puram* poems are all other kinds of poems, usually about good and evil, action, community, kingdom" (Ibidem : 101). Ramanujan's humanistic concerns are evident not only in his creative writings but also in his essays, lectures and translations. The *akam* poetry, synonymous with love poetry in the Tamil tradition, deals with the inner world, the love of man and woman.

In his Introduction to *Hymns for the Drowning : Poems for Vishnu by Nammalvar* Ramanujan explains his method of translation. As he says,

> To translate is to "carry across" : "metaphor" has the same root-meaning. Translations are transpositions; and some elements of the original cannot be transposed at all. For instance, one can often convey a sense of the original rhythm but not the language-bound meter; one

> can mimic levels of diction, even the word play, but not the actual sound of the words (Ramanujan, 1981 : XVI).

In his essay "Classics Lost and Found" Ramanujan says : "The word *translate* is only Latin for the Greek word *metaphor*. Both mean 'carry across'" (*CE* : 189). Despite his awareness of what is lost in translation, Ramanujan largely succeeds in carrying poetry across cultural and linguistic barriers. He quotes John Dryden's description of translation in "The Dedication of Aeneis" as "a kind of drawing after life," steering "betwixt the two extremes of paraphrase and literal translation; to keep as near my author as I could, without losing all his graces, the most eminent of which are in the beauty of his words; and those words, I must add, are always figurative" (Ramanujan, 1981 : xvi).

Ramanujan is a bilingual poet, equally skilful in writing in Kannada and English. Bilingualism and expertise in Linguistics helped him greatly in cultural transmutation. As Bruce King says,

> The highly metaphoric nature of his poetry partly results from an imaginative translation across cultures by striking unexpected associations, a kind of translator's "metaphysical wit" in the creation of multifaceted images. His work as translator and scholar is a strong influence on the mentality that shapes his poetry and his poetics (King : 10).

Despite its rootedness in Indian cultural traditions, Ramanujan's poetry can be read on its own as English-language poetry with modern themes and forms. Thus, he achieves a rare blending of the ancient and the modern, the Indian and the American idioms. As in T.S. Eliot, in Ramanujan too there is continuity from tradition to modernity, a continuity between his poetry, translation, and scholarship.

II

Critics generally look at Ramanujan more as a translator than as a major Indian English poet. But Ramanujan is reported to have said toward the end of his life : "All you have to do is to make it clear that my interest in poetry is central to my being and all my work" (Krishnan, 1993 : 28). As a writer, Ramanujan has not received the kind of recognition that he deserves. A close scrutiny of his *oeuvré* will bring out the variety of his reading and complexity of his creative genius. Bruce King says that Ramanujan's reputation, compared to Ezekiel's or Dom Moraes's, is limited :

> Many critics and Indian poets, including Ezekiel, consider him the best Indian poet but he has not had the same general recognition and following as Moraes and Ezekiel, except for his translation from classical Tamil and Kannada (King : 8).

In fact, Ramanujan's intellectual background and involvement with Indian culture are certainly deeper than Ezekiel's and Moraes's. Even though Ramanujan deals with classical Tamil and Kannada writings, he is at home with the larger Indian ethos. Nissim Ezekiel says :

> India is simply my environment. A man can do something for and in his environment by being fully what he is, by not withdrawing from it. I have not withdrawn from India (Ezekiel : 88).

The tension in Ezekiel between his Bene-Israel roots and his Indian "environment" is evident in his writings, but he does not make conscious attempts to relive his past. Unlike Ezekiel, for Ramanujan despite his "environment" in the U.S., with his roots in India, he is equally involved with both the cultures. For him the American environment is the "exterior" and the Indian environment the "interior." They are the "two lobes" of his brain, as he says in an anecdote about his father (*CE* : 36). As Ramanujan says,

> English and my disciplines (linguistics, anthropology) give me my outer forms — linguistic, metrical, logical and other such ways of shaping experience; and my first thirty years in India, my frequent visits and field trips, my professional preoccupations with Kannada and Tamil, and folklore give me my substance, my "inner" forms, images and symbols. They are continuous with each other, and I no longer can tell what comes from where (Cited in Parthasarathy : 95-96).

Referring to the formative influences of Tamil poets on him, Ramanujan says that in their writings he discovered :

> ...the landscapes, the personae, the appropriate moods, all become a language within language. Like a native speaker, he makes "infinite use of finite means," to say with familiar words what has been said before; he can say exactly what he wants to, without even being aware of the ground-rules of his grammar (Ramanujan, 1967 : 114-15).

Ramanujan is also indebted to Kannada Bhakti poets. As he says,

> The traditional tune-beat, like the ritual gesture, was felt to be learned, passive, inorganic, too well organized to be organic. Here, too, the stharava, the standing thing shall fall, but the jangama shall prevail (Ramanujan, 1973 : 38).

These shaping influences from Indian culture, coupled with the Western influences, have contributed to the complexity of Ramanujan's poetic genius.

As Bruce King says, "His Indianness is a part of his past, [with which] he is inextricably linked as he changes and develops" (King : 8). It is continuity, not conflict for the poet. In the words of Ramanujan, "Just as our biological past lives in the physical body, our social and cultural past lives in the many cultural bodies that we inherit — our languages, arts, religions, and life-cycle rites" (*CE* : 184). Like his biological past, the poet's cultural past continues to live. It is all the more palpable in Ramanujan due to his frequent visits to India in addition to his continued intellectual preoccupation with Indian culture while in the U.S. S. Nagarajan's statement about Ramanujan's "uprootedness" since he is a "marginalized" man sounds commonplace and naive : "The poet is haunted by a sense of irrecoverable loss and of the transitoriness and insubstantiality of his uprooted life. It is the poetry of the marginal man par excellence" (Nagarajan : 786). Nagarajan has surely missed the essential Ramanujan. Nagarajan's view about Ramanujan's "alienation" is similar to S.G. Jainapur's : "There is a deep sense of alienation in his poetry... He felt intensely about his cultural roots when he began to live on alien soil.

This seems to have pushed him back to a Hindu ethos in his poetry" (Jainapur : 108-09). These commonplace statements of critics only betray a lack of proper understanding of the complex genius of Ramanujan who has successfully brought together the Indian and the Western sensibilities.

The modernist English influences of Ezra Pound and T.S. Eliot helped Ramanujan to avoid the abstractions of the post-Independence Indian English verse. In *Second Sight* he successfully fuses the forms and tropes derived from poets like William Carlos Williams, Wallace Stevens, and W.B. Yeats with the traditions of ancient Tamil and medieval Kannada poetry. Ramanujan avoids the "monism" of the "pan-Indian Sanskritic Great Tradition" since he believes that "cultural traditions in India are indissolubly plural and often conflicting" (*CE* : 8). As he asserts, "India does not have one past, but many pasts" (*CE* : 187).

As Jahan Ramazani says, referring to Ramanujan :

> Like the postcolonial or migrant subject, torn out of one cultural context and inserted into a new one, the eye that blinks in a new head or the heart that beats in a new chest cannot always adapt with ease to its new surroundings (Ramazani : 43).

It is difficult to put Ramanujan's writing in the straight jacket of postcoloniality. Terms like "displacement," "transfer," "migration," and "alienation" are typical of the postcolonial studies. Ramanujan is certainly an exception as a writer functioning in an alien climate containing both the Eastern and the Western sensibilities within himself. As he says in an interview,

> The past never passes, either the individual past or historical past or cultural past. It is with us...the disconnection is as much an understanding of the past as making the connection. And the living in the present have to see both (Jha : 7-8).

Central to Ramanujan's vision is continuity, past and present, tradition and modernity acting on each other endlessly. Gayatri Chakravorty Spivak says that cultural reversal and displacement results in "the binary opposition, the Western intellectual's longing for all that is not West, ...the so-called non-West's turn toward the West" (Spivak : 8). Ramanujan is unique in his ability to contain within himself the binaries, explaining the East to the West and the West to the East with perfect equanimity.

Ramanujan is opposed to the "hypocrisy" of the Indian mind on account of his great concern for the true Indian values. In "Prayers to Lord Murugan," he laments the dichotomy between the inner culture and the outer manifestations : "our blood is brown/our collars white," both in contrast to the Red God :

> Lord of the sixth sense
> give us back
> our five senses...
>
> Deliver us O presence
> from proxies
> and absences
> from Sanskrit and the mythologies
> of night and the several
> roundtable mornings
>
> of London and return
> the future to what
> it was. (*CP* : 117)

Ramanujan rejects the abstract and the spiritual in preference to the realities of the Indian life. He wants to highlight the real India free from old myths, abstraction of dead languages and high-falutin talk about political gatherings like the Round Table Conference in London. Ramanujan uses irony to comment on the falsehood of modern Indian mementoes and legends like rajas posing for photographs standing over tigers, and legends like "the peacocks we sent in the Bible/to Solomon."

As an Indian English poet, Ramanujan is unique in integrating the Indian and the Western images. Referring to "Prayers to Lord Murugan," he says that it "could not have been written if I did not know Classical Tamil forms, and even some of the images there" (Jha, 1981 : 7). He also stresses the importance of the forms of Classical Tamil poetry and how he tried to adapt those forms in his English poems :

> I prefer the Classical. A typical "Sangam" poem has well-defined, well-wrought complex form. It has an articulate body of convention behind it. The image is not flaunted here but is sharp and pointed (Nakulan : 11).

In his use of the Classical Tamil forms, Ramanujan prefers sharpness of the images. In his English poetry, this use of language is fused with its modern Western counterpart. It is like the use of images by T.S. Eliot and Ezra Pound. In the first section of "Prayers to Lord Murugan," Ramanujan deals with the deep sense of loss in the modern world because Lord Murugan has lost significance in a spiritually bankrupt world. These images of the spiritual bankruptcy of the modern world remind of the images used by T.S. Eliot in *The Waste Land.* As Edward C. Dimock, Jr., says, in "Prayers to Lord Murugan" Ramanujan attempts "to use human and concrete forms to express the ultimate yet intimate nature of the religious experience" (Demock, Jr : 170). This "religious experience" is not abstract but related to the modern existence.

In one of his interviews, Ramanujan talks about his use of language in poetry and also the plastic quality of poetry :

> Everybody uses language, yet when I use it, I must use it in such a way that it says something new, innocent. Language is full of stock phrases, cliches — you fall back on them whenever you are really thinking. It is exactly like perception...The words, when they appear in a particular order, surprise you, as though you had never seen them before. That's when you know you can't change it any more (Dasgupta : 33).

The sharpness of the image in Ramanujan's poetry is not only like the one in Classical Tamil poetry, but also in the Western writing, as in Ezra Pound's poetry. As Ezra Pound says, "Image is more than an Idea. It is a vortex or cluster of fused ideas and is endowed with energy" (Pound : 349). If we accept the fact that Ramanujan's poem is replete with images, we shall acknowledge the presence of multiple ideas in it, particularly due to his multicultural vision. In the manifesto of the Imagist Movement, published in 1913, Pound emphasizes : "(1) Direct treatment of the 'thing' whether subjective or objective; (2) To use absolutely no word that did not contribute to the presentation" (Cited in Coffman, Jr : 141). Also, in a companion article signed by Pound there is an interesting elaboration : "An 'Image' is that which presents an intellectual and emotional complex in an instant of time" (Ibidem). According to S. Nagarajan, there is distortion of ideas and limitation of the range of feelings in Ramanujan's use of images since there are different levels of achievement in the same poem (Cited in Dwivedi : 128). What Nagarajan seems to take as a deficiency in Ramanujan is actually multiplicity of meaning in the poet. Bruce King is more convincing when he says, "His poetry is rich in images and cultural echoes — words reflect and interact with other words — a wide variety of associations from more than one culture and from various historical periods" (King : 8). Thus, what is significant in Ramanujan's images is the cultural resonance, not limitation of the range of feeling. This multiplicity of meaning in Ramanujan's images is the result of his deep involvement with both the Indian and American cultures in addition to his wide-ranging scholarship in cultural anthropology and folklores.

Parthasarathy refers to Ramanujan's "eye for the specific physiognomy of an object or a situation which he then reveals with telling detail" (Parthasarathy : 95). This eye for detail results in the concreteness of the image. In "The Striders" Ramanujan presents the concrete New England water-bug image :

> This bug sits
> on a landslide of lights
> and drowns eye —
> deep
> into its tiny strip
> of sky.

In "Small Scale Reflections on the Great House" the poet's cataloguing of details like "lame wandering cows," "sons-in-law," "letters" (*CP* : 96-99) or in "Elements of Composition", "memory," "millennia of fossils," etc. (*CP* : 122) is evidently the result of his scholarly involvement with anthropology. For Ramanujan, "memory" is not confined to the family only, or to something that happened in the present or the past. It is anthropological :

I pass through them
as they pass through me
taking and leaving
affections, seeds, skeletons
millennia of fossils records
of insects that do not last
a day. (*CP* : 122)

This is how Ramanujan is able to bring his scholarship in anthropology to his observation of life around him.

According to Niranjan Mohanty, "Ramanujan's poetry should not be assumed to have originated from the Hindu or Indian milieu, it should rather be seen from the perspective of the symbiosis of the 'outer' and the 'inner' substances" (Mohanty: 177). It will be more appropriate to say that while the Hindu or Indian milieu constitutes the "inner" substance of Ramanujan's poetry, the Western milieu shapes the "outer" substance, the two co-existing. In "Extended Family," Ramanujan compares family members and cultures (*CP* : 169-170). The naked, bathing speaker rediscovers himself in relation to others :

Yet like grandfather
I bathe before the village crow
the dry chlorine water
my only Ganges
the naked Chicago bulb
a cousin of the Vedic sun.

Ramanujan brings together the Chicago bulb and the Vedic sun. America is to India what the speaker is to his grandfather. The chlorinated urban water and a sacred river are juxtaposed in an urbanized and Americanized setting. The poem symbolizes Ramanujan's own status as a member of an "extended family," living simultaneously in different cultures and writing about them.

In "A Poem on Particulars" Ramanujan shows how various trees are connected with the lineage of a "single orange." He suggests that one should be reconciled to the world of flux. As a Hindu married to a Syrian Christian and living in America, Ramanujan is aware of the colonial and postcolonial conflicts. His poems reveal his awareness that the past and the present constantly interact, reminding us of Eliot's "Tradition and the

Individual Talent." In "History" Ramanujan shows change as a perspective. The speaker as an adult remembers his childhood. The poem takes the reader into the midst of an action. History becomes a reality of the present. "Small-scale Reflections on a Great House" brings history close to the present. The house is a past, a memory, a tradition.

Continuity is a term that is applicable to Ramanujan's works — within a specific genre like poetry or its relation to others like folklore, language, cultural anthropology. Ramanujan exemplifies the extension of the cultural past into the present not only at the specific Indian level but also the universal. Herein lies his uniqueness as a theorist and writer par excellence.

WORKS CITED

Blackburn, Stuart H. and A.K. Ramanujan (Eds.) 1986. *Another Harmony : New Essays on the Folklore of India.* New Delhi : Oxford Univ. Press.

Coffman, Stanley K., Jr. 1951. *Imagism : A Chapter for the History of Modern Poetry.* Norman : Univ. of Oklahoma Press.

Dasgupta, Chidanand. 1983. "Suddenly a Phrase Begins to Sing," *Span,* 24, 11 (November) : 32-34.

Dimock, Edward C., Jr. 1974. *The Literatures of India : An Introduction.* Chicago : Univ. of Chicago Press.

Dwivedi, A.N. 1995. *The Poetic Art of A.K. Ramanujan.* New Delhi : B.R. Publishing Corporation.

Ezekiel, Nissim, 1974. "Naipaul's India and Mine" in Adil Jussawalla (ed.) *New Writing in India.* Harmondsworth : Penguin.

Hymes, Dell. 1972. "The Contribution of Folklore to Sociolinguistic Research" in Americao Parades and Richard Rauman (eds.) *Toward New Perspectives in Folklore.* Austin : Univ. of Texas Press.

Jainapur, S.G. 1987. *Poetry, Culture and Language : Indo-Anglian Poets from Karnataka.* Calcutta : Writers Workshop.

Jha, Rama. 1981. "A Conversation with A.K. Ramanujan." *Humanitics Press,* 3, 1 : 5-13.

King, Bruce, 1991. *Three Indian Poets.* New Delhi : Oxford Univ. Press.

Krishnan, S. 1993. "A Poet's Quest". *Indian Review of Books,* 2, 11 (Aug. 16-Sept. 15) : 28.

Mohanty, Niranjan. 1993. "Things as They Are : The Poetry of A.K. Ramanujan." *Journal of South Asian Literature,* 28, 182 : (Spring & Fall) : 167-80.

Nagarjan, S. 1991. "A.K. Ramanujan" in Tracy Chevalier (ed.) *Contemporary Poets.* Chicago : St. James Press.

Nakulan. 1969. "A Meeting with A.K. Ramanujan." *Thought*, 21, 48 : 11-13.

Parthasarathy, R. (ed.) 1976. *Ten Twentieth-Century Indian Poets*. New Delhi : Oxford Univ. Press.

Pound, Ezra. 1915. "Affirmations." *The New Age* : 16 : 13 (Jan. 28) : 349.

Ramanujan, A.K. 1999. *The Collected Essays of A.K. Ramanujan* (ed.) Vinay Dharwadker. New Delhi : Oxford Univ. Press. Referred to as *CE* in the text.

———. 1995. *The Collected Poems of A.K. Ramanujan* (ed.) Vinay Dharwadker. New Delhi : Oxford Univ. Press. Referred to as *CP* in the text.

———. 1993. *Folklores from India : A Selection of Oral Tales from Twenty Two Languages*. New Delhi : Penguin India.

———. 1981. *The Hymns for the Drowning*. New Delhi : Penguin India.

———. 1967. *The Interior Landscape*. Bloomington : Indiana Univ. Press.

———. 1973. *Speaking of Siva*. London : Penguin.

Ramazani, Jahan, 1998. "Metaphor and Postcoloniality : The Poetry of A.K. Ramanujan." *Contemporary Literature* : 39, 1 (Spring) : 27-53.

Said, Edward. 1978. *Orientalism*. London : Routledge & Kegan Paul.

Spivak, Gayatri Chakravorty. 1990. *The Post-Colonial Critic : Interviews, Strategies, Dialogues*. New York : Routledge.

2

Correcting a Critical Fallacy : A Closer Reading of Ramanujan's Three Early Poems

—*SURYA NATH PANDEY*

A major fallacy in respect of the poetry of A.K. Ramanujan has perhaps been about his poems written in India, prior to his visit to USA on a Fulbright Fellowship in 1958, where he eventually settled down. We have an authentic information (see Appendix B) that he proceeded abroad with a batch of significant poems[1], a fact also borne out by the poet's own admission, "actually my first poems were published in the *Illustrated Weekly, Quest* and *Thought* in 1955" (Ramanujan 1980 : III). Since these poems could be collected together only in *The Striders* (1966) and *Relations* (1971) during his stay in Chicago (though quite a few are still uncollected), the critics, even those with

1. They include 'Still Another View of Grace,' 'A Hindu to His Body,' 'Self-Portrait,' 'Anxiety' and 'Conventions of Despair' collected in *The Striders*; 'Army Ants,' 'Eyes, Ears, Noses, and a Thing about Touch' and 'Smalltown, South India' published in *Relations;* 'No Dream, No Symbol', 'The Body as the Translator,' 'Of Corruption,' 'Madura : Two Movements' and 'The Gnomes' still uncollected in Ramanujan's verse-volumes. Moreover, 'I Listened,' 'Carpe Diem,' 'the Whip,' 'The Past,' 'Two Days,' 'Of Curves' and 'Stranger' are also among his uncollected poems. May be some of them (except 'Stranger') were written in fifties.

   Bruce King also observes, "By the early 1960s, before he went to the United States, he had a book-length manuscript ready. A friend showed it to an editor at Oxford University Press in India who, as Oxford India did not then publish any poetry, sent it on to England" — *Three Indian Poets* (Madras : Oxford University Press, 1991), p. 11.

acknowledged credentials and celebrity images have treated them as products of the poet's cross-cultural interactions, which is obviously a travesty of truth. The present author nurses, in all modesty, an apprehension that Ramanujan's poetry has been viewed with a preconceived notion that whatever is remarkable about his creativity is invariably an outcome of his exposure to the West. A slightly cautious study of his early poetry demonstrates that quite a few of these pieces seem to be programme-poems charting out the future course of Ramanujan's poetry. His visit abroad simply reaffirmed his initial convictions which acquired greater poignancy and sharpness during his stay in America. The present paper intends to examine three of these early poems — 'Self-Portrait,' 'Conventions of Despair,' and 'Still Another View of Grace' — in their proper contexts. The very titles of these poems betray the poet's typical mindset — existential angst and question of identity — at the time of his departure to States where his inbuilt predilections achieved such exuberance and vivacity as never before.

'Self-Portrait' (*CP* : 23) is one of the earliest poems of Ramanujan written sometimes in early fifties though included in *The Striders* (1966) for the first time. One of he neatest pieces in his poetic *oeuvré*, it centres in the poet's obsessive preoccupation with self-questioning which developed into a rigorous discipline with the passage of time and subsumed in its ken everything associated with him — his family, his caste, his inherited religious dogmas and so on. The poem takes up the question of his individual identity in an apparently innocent manner with the opening lines sounding paradoxical :

> I resemble everyone
> but myself, and sometimes see
> in shop-windows,
> despite the well-known laws
> of optics,
> the portrait of a stranger,
> date unknown,
> often signed in a corner
> by my father.

(*CP*: 23)

The unlikeness between 'I' and 'myself' is so startling that the persona's image reflected in shop-windows assails him as "the portrait of a stranger." Obviously this contrast defies the principles of optics which propound that 'image is reflection of real.' In a later *Relations* piece "Real Estate," the poet amends for himself, as it were, the laws of light :

He always knew
glass was good. 'It's rational,
it reflects'...
Yet refracts
all things for the man within,
defining some men in, others out,
with apparent transparency. (*CP* : 91)

The disparity gets explained that the 'shop-windows' act in mysterious ways, sometimes reflect and sometimes refract as well. The stranger-image has two modifiers which are intimately connected with each other, and help us decipher his whereabouts. Since this picture bears the authentication of persona's father, this similarity threatens to obliterate his identity. However, the phrase 'signed in a corner' undermines father's influence as marginal overtly because the signature is not across the photograph if one chooses to read it literally. And at the same time it also indicates the protagonist's receptivity to multiple reflections and opacities (One recalls Ramanujan's oft-quoted statement — "English and my disciplines...and I no longer can tell what comes from where." Cited in Parthasarathy : 96).

Chirantan Kulshrestha reads here the unavoidable compulsion of being "what one is one's father's son, absurdly destined to assume an identity attached to oneself by forces beyond one's control" (Kulshrestha : 178). The protagonist is musing over his individual predicament and to treat it as a general observation on the fate of all children seems to be off the point. The learned critic ignores the adverb of time 'often' to reach at an inference incompatible with the context. True, father as the head of the family is one of the traditional guideposts of identity but a child achieves his distinctiveness by virtue of his innate traits which may or may not tally with his father's. Moreover, this comment also creates the impression that the persona is tired of his personality being eroded by his father's, which is again a fact liable to be contested. By tactfully employing the 'stranger image,' with the rider 'often' Ramanujan admits of areas of connections as well as contrasts between the two immediate generations which have many an occasion to rub shoulders with. Candidly referring to his own experience, Ramanujan writes :

> I had just been converted by Russell to the 'Scientific attitude.' I (and my generation) was troubled by his [father's] holding together in one brain both astronomy and astrology; I looked for consistency in him, a consistency he didn't seem to care about, or even think about ("Is There an Indian Way of Thinking? An Informal Essay," *CE* : 36).

One can appreciate Ramanujan's search for 'consistency' in his father's personality which explicitly combined rationality and irrationality, in terms of 'generation gap.' Incidentally he uses the term 'my generation' and speaks as a spokesman of his group, forgetting by the way, that the generation of his father also had a specific set of values and as such, it was perfectly within its rights to go the way it pleased. However, there are moments when preferences clash and the younger generation has to give in. One learns that Ramanujan's father put his hands down regarding the choice of his son's disciplines and "literally took him [Ramanujan] by the hand in the Registrar's office and changed his major from Science to English" because he thought his son "not mathematically minded" (*CE* : 16). If "signed in a corner/by my father" points to the weaknesses like inconsistency in Ramanujan's personality, it also underlines with equal force the humanistic strain so pronounced in his poetry, a result of his exposure to literature and humanities.

Ramanujan's confession of sharing his father's attributes 'often' prompts one to note those very traits to assess their degree of resemblance or otherwise. In a typically jocular vein he talks of his father's peculiar way of bathing — "...in brothers'/ anecdotes of how noisily/father bathed/slapping soap on his back;...? ('Love Poem for a Wife I,' *CP* : 65) and also of his knack of riddles and proverbs — "sky-man in a man-hole/...fat man full of proverbs/the language of lean years..." ('Astronomer,'

CP : 134). Conceding that everyman is a bathroom singer, this is obviously an unsophisticated way of taking bath, but Ramanujan imitates his father in Chicago apartment — "slap soap on my back/like father/and think/in proverbs" (Extended Family,' *CP*: 169). While his father bathed noisily chanting hymns and *shlokas*, in the toilet, he is considerate — "he [simply] think/in proverbs" — lest the privacy of others might be disturbed. He not only 'thinks in proverbs' he has gone a step ahead and published his first book in Kannada under the title *Proverbs* (1955). Then follow the lines which demarcate the difference between their habits :

> like me
> I wipe myself dry
> with an unwashed
> Sears turkish towel. (*CP* : 169)

It might have been disgusting and unthinkable, from the father's point of view to use an 'unwashed and spotted towel' to cleanse oneself after bath, but the son in his usual way continues with his old habits, probably because they die hard. This is a marginal improvement or otherwise on a father's over-riding influence.

'Signed.../by my father' may also be construed as voicing Ramanujan's unhappiness over patriarchal values.[2] One remembers telling him in 'Elements of Composition' :

> Composed as I am, like others,
> of elements on certain well-known lists,
> father's seed and mother's egg... (*CP* : 12)

It is certainly not a coincidence that his second volume *Relations* features on its cover a stark photograph of the author's face, his forehead pictured with an inset photograph of his parents, literally on his mind as it were. To a suggestion to remove the inset photograph, Ramanujan quipped that "the remaining prospect, that of a cover filled by his own naked face, was an even worse alternative" (*CE* : XV). It is more than a symbolic

2. For a detailed critique see Surya Nath Pandey, "Feminist Concerns in Ramanujan's Poetry," *Journal of Indian Writing in English,* 26, 2 (July 1998), 14-25. Also in his *Studies in Contemporary Poets* (New Delhi : Atlantic, 1999), p. 91-101.

gesture, and can be properly appreciated only within the Indian cultural framework.

In his poetry, the poet has made no secret of his animus against the male members of his pedigree including his father at various places — "after quarrelling/with my father about my mother's rights..." ('On Not Learning from Animals,' *CP* : 217), and "At times, the wobbly top father gave me/quietly after we both had a tantrum"...('A Wobbly Top,' *CP* : 60) — one has reasons to look for feminist bias here, though far-fetched and only partially convincing. His fault-finding in his father's personality has still another dimension for which he coaxes him in 'Obituary' supposedly written to mourn the irreparable loss :

everything he didn't quite
manage to do himself,
like his caesarian birth
in a brahmin ghetto
and his death by heart
failure in the fruit market. (*CP* : 112)

The father, A.A. Krishnaswami's failure to manipulate his birth somewhere outside 'a brahmin ghetto' has earned him his illustrious son's diatribe at several places in his writings. The father-identification, an absent presence, gave his profile certain attributes he felt embarrassed by. However, the yoking together of 'fruit market' with 'brahmin ghetto' lends a humorous aura to the supposedly serious content of the piece. Connections and contrasts between original and copy engage the poet also in a later poem "Drafts."

Ramanujan does not regard only his portrait as stranger's, he even treats his real self likewise in the poem rightly titled 'Stranger' written in his fiftyninth year (though not included in his *Collected Poems*) :

at finding myself
alien, with a ghost
of a moustache with a wisp
of bear foam
in a familiar house.

(Ramanujan, 1990-91 : 38)

This tendency further extends in respect of his wife also who becomes "the faraway/stranger who's nearby" and thus permitting him greater freedom :

> ...so I can play son,
> father, brother, macho lover, gaping
> tourist, and clumsy husband.
>
> ('Love Poem for a Wife and Her Trees,' *CP* : 183)

'Self-Portrait' has been misread by some scholars including N.L. Sharma who looks for American influence here, almost a decade before the poet embarked for Indiana :

> ...he admits in 'Self-Portrait' such crisis of identity and identification in the beginning of his stay in the States...such imagery ['shop-windows'] is revealing of the initial impact of the American cultural milieu and literature on the mind of this Indo-American poet (Sharma : 181).

That the poet experienced a split personality whether in India or in America is testified to by the use of his 'favourite image' in one of his later poems also :

> till mirrors in a mirror-shop
> break me up into how many I was
> show me in profile and fragment...
>
> ('Not Knowing,' *CP* : 216)

The context gets all the more horrible when a critic traces confusion in the poet's mental make-up due to exposure, even in a piece pointedly subtitled 'A Second Look at Ramanujan's Poetry' :

> He goes West and absorbs a new ethos...This results in a confusion of values and consequent loss of identity [in 'Self-Portrait'] : he is not at home in his new surroundings and at the same time is sceptical of the Indian mores which had been inculcated into him in his childhood (Sengupta : 83).

The question of personal identity assumes a much larger dimension in "Conventions of Despair" where the dilemma of the outsider and the marginal man is taken up at length.

"Conventions of Despair" (*CP* : 34-35), one of Ramanujan's

longest early poems was written in 1957 in Pune during his sojourn at Deccan College for a Diploma course in linguistics. It is a central piece in that it encapsulates the poet's major thematic and stylistic concerns overtly anticipating several of Ramanujan's well-known poems *viz.*, 'A Hindu to His Body,' 'The Hindoo : he doesn't hurt a fly or a spider either,' 'The Hindoo : he reads his Gita and is calm at all events,' 'The Hindoo : the only risk,' and 'Second Sight' among others. Written in a typical Ramanujan *tri-padi* (three line stanza), a form in which *Speaking of Siva* was translated partly in India and which was to become his most favourite stanza pattern in years to come, 'Conventions of Despair' begins in the midst of an argument which has engaged the poet persona for quite some time. There seems to have been an upsetting tussle in the poet's psyche between the values of modernism and those of asceticism, each trying to get the better of other. And thus enjoining upon the poet to take the hard decision either in favour of the devil or the deep sea. Since the poet presents two sets of attitudes, quite a few scholars teat this poem as a product of uprootedness. While K.R. Rao feels :

> It is obvious that Ramanujan operates altogether with a different sensibility and writes as a displaced Indian, and not as an Indian appropriating the other orders of experience (Rao, 1997 : 104).

P. Mallikarjuna Rao takes up 'Conventions of Despair' to write his critical piece "The Poetry of Exile : A Study of A.K. Ramanujan" (Rao, 1996 : 64). He obviously treats the term 'exile' to mean one physically dislocated from his roots. These two critics hailing from Andhra Pradesh look for expatriation, displacement and polarity in a poem which was written in their neighbouring state of Maharashtra. However, one recalls that Ezra Pound had also used the term 'exile' to mean 'inner immigration,' while explicating the term 'Patria' but these scholars have certainly not employed the word in that specific sense.

The poet begins the piece on an emphatic note underlining his awareness of the contemporary reality with its fashionable attitudinizing and intellectual patronising. He is aware of the necessity of joining the mainstream lest one might be dubbed 'the Outsider' or 'the Marginal Man.' As he is narrating the unconventionality of modernism, something pricks him :

> But, sorry, I cannot unlearn
> Conventions of despair.
> They have their pride.

Despite the dangers that await one refusing to be modernised, the persona reiterates politely that "I cannot unlearn/Conventions of despair." One feels that there is a solid ground for his not getting scared of despair emboldened by his father's advice as he is :

> Just comb your hair.
> You shouldn't worry about Despair
> Despair is a strange disease.
> I think it happens even to trees.
> ('Despair' — 'Excerpts from a Father's Wisdom,'
> *CP* : 41)

Armed with his father's sagacity, the poet treats 'despair' as part of the game called 'life' since all flora and fauna in the macrocosm are unavoidably its potential victims. Such a conviction instills a qualitative change in human perception and to that extent 'Conventions of Despair' have their pride of place in mundane existence. Then follow probably the most commented upon lines :

> I must seek and will find
> my particular hell only in my hindu mind;...

The ideas of hell and heaven weigh very heavily on the Hindu psyche — "of every punishment/in the narrow woodcut columns/ of the yellowing almanacs of Hindu hells' (*CP* : 148) — and this brings in the concept of *Karma.* In his essay "Is There an Indian Way of Thinking? An Informal Essay," Ramanujan precisely defines *Karma* as

> a notion that is almost synonymous in some circles with whatever is Indian or Hindu. Brahmanical texts had it, the Buddhists had it, the Jainas had it...*Karma* implies the self's past determining the present an iron chain of cause and consequence, an ethic of responsibility (*CE* : 37).

This 'ethic of responsibility' is a matter of serious concern, an inescapable calamity and one has to come to terms with it in one's own way. The quantum of punishment awarded to a sinner is in proportion to his sins accumulating since past lives and it varies from person to person. Of the seven varieties of hell, the worst is *kumbhipāka,* a place full of puss all around. When the persona says 'my particular hell,' he is conscious of the magnitude of suffering his accumulated sins might have in store for him. Ramanujan mentions concept of *talaividi* ('headwriting') also commonly believed by Hindus as a possible explanation of their earthly sufferings. "*Talaividi*" writes the poet, "is one's fate inscribed arbitrarily at one's birth on one's forehead; the inscription has no relation to one's prior actions; usually in such explanations (and folktales about them) past lives are not even part of the scheme" (*CE* : 37-38). Whether caused by *karma* or improvised by *talaividi,* Ramanujan's rider 'only' to 'my hindu mind' decides the parametres which might determine the nature of his cognitions and concerns. The use of the lower capital 'h' in Hindu underlines his revisionist approach to the inherited faith which singles him out from his brethren who accept tradition unquestionably. The use of the modals 'must' and 'will' underscores the unavoidability of the predicament and also the virtue of fortitude that best defines the protagonist's personal make up. Be as it is, Ramanujan continues to be a Hindu planning out his future within the broad framework of his ancestral faith. Incidentally these principal verbs — 'seek,' 'find' — appear with equal potency in another spiritual context in the last piece of *Collected Poems,* "Fear No Fall." The poet recalls how the great Tamil Saint Arunagiri's life witnessed altogether a different routine once he found himself in the lap of 'The Old Man' *i.e.*, his god Murugan. His life had previously been unbearably miserable — "His despair, deeper than his wounds" — but all this suffered a sea-change :

> leaving Arunagiri a lifetime
> of seeking and finding and losing Him
> again and again in a labyrinth
> of winding words,... (*CP* : 276)

Sujit S. Dulai mistakenly opines that such a crucial decision was possible for the persona only under alien influence :

> The protagonist refuses to give up the solid substance of his foundational self for the fashionable but empty attitudinizing as a pallaiative in his new, modern and difficult environment (Dulai : 153).

Having identified his perspective, Ramanujan unravells other layers of his 'particular hell' in the latter half of the poem. He is inclined to undergo experiences of a normal man, without subjecting himself to the rigours of an ascetic life. He is reluctant to exchange the present for some rosy future — "the theory of a peacock-feathered future," as he calls it. Not that he is unmindful of the afflictions of life, but he vehemently maintains his stand :

> No, no, give me back my archaic despair :
> It's not obsolete yet to live
> in this many-lived lair
> of fears, this flesh.

One recalls Ramanujan remembering his father's 'warning' — "The body is not easy to wear" ('Excerpts from a Father's Wisdom,' *CP* : 42) and his resolve is all the more striking under these givens. In fact, the propelling force behind this firm determination is his inherited faith which relegates body to spirit — "But/You know my tribe, incarnate/unbelievers in bodies,..." ('Death and the Good Citizen,' *CP* : 136).

This rambling of despair has been misjudged even by no less a critic than G.N. Devy also while building up his thesis of alienation. He reads external determinants in Ramanujan's situation :

> Alienation, in Ramanujan's poetry, cuts both ways : he is alienated from the Indian ethos as well as from the life in Chicago (as 'Conventions of Despair' would show...). (Devy : 19)

The last poem chosen for discussion 'Still Another View of Grace' (*CP* : 45) was originally published under the title 'A Poem on Logic' in *Quest* (Feb.-March 1958, p. 38). Like the two pieces discussed earlier, this poem has also been read out of context. The most amazing (read shocking) comment comes from the editor of *Ten Twentieth-Century Indian Poets,* R. Parthasarathy, who in his introductory note on Ramanujan observes :

> For the past fifteen years, he has lived in the United States...India and America tend to exist separately, and come together, however, only at a time of personal crisis explored, for instance, in "Still Another View of Grace" (Parthasarathy : 95).

By 'a time of personal crisis,' Parthasarathy intends to trace autobiographical strain in the poem born out of Ramanujan's marriage with Molly Daniels, a Syrian Christian. However there is no question of his American experience coming to his rescue since the poet had hardly crossed the Black Waters by that time.

The poet persona adopts a dramatic overture to register his protest against certain values of his inherited faith. The title implies that there are no absolute concepts and tenets and that things can be viewed from various angles with equal ease and confidence. Ramanujan had been seriously reading and, sometimes translating as well *Vecanas* of medieval Kannada saint poets at this time and his translations finally appeared as *Speaking of Siva* (1973). Their ideas might have struck his sensitive mind as to the social anomalies eating into the very vitals of our cultural framework. As a young man he reacted to the contemporary scenario in 'another way,' pronouncedly different from the conformist character of society just as the *Vacanakaras* before him had done centuries ago. The opening line — "I burned and burned" — underlines the perturbing nature of the dilemma which has been upsetting him for quite some time — his outrage against social norms that deny equality on counts of colour, caste and creed. If one looks at his poetry, there is a history of his getting disturbed by issues that possess him in entirety — "And that woman.....she will not let me rest..." ('Still Another for Mother,' *CP* : 15); 'I Could Have Rested' (*CP* : 15). When the anguish reached the stage of the proverbial last straw on the camel's back, "But one day I turned — and caught that thought/by the screens of her hair...." One can discreetly note that there was nothing impulsive or impetuous about his action as it was well-pondered over and leisurely meditated upon. The original title

'A Poem on Logic' intends to dispel any such misapprehensions the reader might nurse about the protagonist being eccentric. The speaker opens his volley of arguments against the accepted values while addressing the mental image of a low-caste girl in a commanding tone :

> 'Beware.
> Do not follow a gentleman's morals
> with that absurd determined air.
> Find a priest. Find any beast in the wind
> for a husband. He will give you a houseful
> of legitimate sons...

It is a clarion call to challenge 'gentleman's morals' which have no logic behind them. The persona's outrage explodes in monosyllables — "Find a priest. Find any beast in the wind"... — which underscore the urgency of action. He seems to suggest that whoever happens to come her way — 'priest' or beast" — she must rope in as a potential husband, ignoring his accomplishments or otherwise. Patrician or plebian, sophisticated or primitive, he will provide her security in the eyes of the society. At this point, logic again intrudes justifying this apparently unconventional decision since it will guarantee "a houseful/of legitimate sons."

Having advanced a candid advice to the girl to be on the lookout for a husband, the poet persona analyses the suitability of his own person as an alternative. Given his 'case history' (to borrow the term from the very title of one of his poems in *Collected Poems* : 47), his propensity to free sex is quite plausible. In an extremely normal upbringing he has hardly experienced any thrills of perversities except "one kiss under the stairs." But the lines which follow, present his true profile :

> Once he ran
> from a body-house without windows
> looking for the wombs of faceless women
>
> he never filled
> with sons. ('Case History,' *CP* : 47)

This credential prompts him to ponder over the possible consequences of his tying a knot with the girl, coming as he does form an upper-caste family. However, rationality takes the better of the dictates of social system — and he cares a fig for it — "It is too late for sin/even for treason." The use of words 'sin' and 'treason' demonstrates protagonist's unimpeded resolve. 'Sin' has implications for the life hereafter while 'treason' refers to the punishment of here and now. He further indicates that he is hardly bothered to ascertain her community, while looking for a suitable match whether in conformity with family traditions or otherwise. He elaborates on his cloistered and stiflingly conservative background and also on his individual priorities :

> Bred Brahmin among singers of shivering hymns
> I shudder to the bone at hungers that roam the street
> beyond the constable's beat.'

Born of Shri Vaishnavite Brahmin parents devoted to reciting hymns (which prompted Ramanujan to translate *Hymns for the Drowning : Poems for Visnu* by Nammalvar (1981), the poet does shudder to the bone, but on different considerations. He has not forgiven his father for being born "in a brahmin ghetto" in 'Obituary' which compulsorily plunged him into an environment, most unsuited to his temperament. He had to struggle hard to overcome an inbuilt moral normalcy but K. Chellappan and his fellow collaborator in their collective wisdom look for cultural encounter here :

> In the poem 'Still Another View of Grace," we see an Indian sensibility encountering the American milieu and enriching the experience through irony. The syntax and vocabulary are predominantly Indian...but they are brought into a creative collaboration with the new milieu (Chellappan : 100).

The poem concludes on a note of revolt. On sighting the girl mentally on a nightlit April, the protagonist defies all moral instructions ingrained in him :

> Commandments crumbled
> in my father's past. Her tumbled hair suddenly known
> as silk in my angry hand, I shook a little
> and took her behind the laws of my land.

The moral scruples prove fragile as the persona catches at her tumbled silky hair flouting the conventional laws of his ancient land. However, a tremor of guilt gripps him shaking 'a little.' The space between the penultimate and the final line does suggest that this shaking was not as insignificant as the modifier 'little' would imply. It rather caused convulsions in the persona's mind since he did something that contravened conservative morality. Notwithstanding all this, the protagonist feels that his was unquestionably a graceful action, though not in strict conformity with the received notions. Rajeev S. Patke, in an otherwise perceptive essay, treats this defiant expression of sexual desire as product of poet's acculturation in the Western milieu, which robbed him of all inhibitions :

> Ramanujan's perception of himself as of Hindu descent provides another internal dimension to this dialogue between the imperious and genetically imprinted demands of the Brahmin within him against which his current limited Western sense of self now defines itself, sometimes defiantly, as say, with the poems on sexual desire (Patke : 117).

However, Bruce King competently notes the burden of Ramanujan's early poems published in *Quest* :

> They show that early on he had a curious relationship to Brahmanism and Indian spirituality. Like a Catholic theologian quarreling [sic] with his church (King, 1993 : Personal Communication).

The foregoing discussion demonstrates that a critical fallacy has infected Ramanujan-criticism to blow up his so-called rootlessness out of all proportions. S.K. Desai goes to the extent of even sounding offensive at this enterprise :

> ...Ramanujan's expatriation is a marginal affair, and thanks to his bilingualism and bicultural living, his alienation is a myth created by theory-loving critics (Desai : 110).

However, even Desai errs in respect of the pieces taken up here when he comments :

> In *The Striders* the poetry of perception dominates, though we see the poet moving towards cognitive tension

> in poems like 'Conventions of Despair,' 'Still Another View of Grace' and 'A Hindu to His Body' (Desai : 116).

The poet is not 'moving towards' rather he begins with tensions caused by the new post-Independence socio-cultural process which included modernisation and a radical change of values during his stay in India itself.

Since Ramanujan believed that "Creativity comes out of sustained attention to one's own experience, one's own locality, one's own environment" (Ramanujan, 1980 : III), he has ridiculed the idea of centre and circumference, as an obnoxious proposition. In the poem ironically titled "Looking for the Centre," he makes fun of this ingenious exercise :

> Looking for the centre these days
> is like looking for the Center
> for Missing Children...
>
> Ask there
> for the Center, anyone will tell you.

The second stanza opens on a still more contemptible note :

> Looking for the Centre is a job
> for eccentrics who can feel the thirteen
> motions of the earth
>
> When they stand still in the middle
> of the market. (*CP* : 184)

The poet feels that in the present times when the world has shrunk into a global village, it is abnormal to think of clinging on simply to one's own inherited ways of cultural preferences. Ramanujan believed that "race, language and culture are three independent variables" and that "neither is any of them pure and single in itself." He elaborates on his own predicament in a posthumously published piece, a lecture initially drafted in 1991 titled "Some Thoughts on 'Non-Western' Classics : With Indian Examples" :

> I was born in South India and I'm here in the United States speaking English, listening to and wanting to understand Chinese poetry, African epics and Caribbean novels. I've students born in Japan, Iowa or Czechoslovakia who learn Tamil or Sanskrit, become

> experts in Zuni rituals or Javanese music. Who is to keep us from breaking out of labels like Indian, WASP, Wog or Korean? (*CE* : 117).

The above explanation might create the impression that this perception is extremely personal born of his own situation. But towards the end of the same essay Ramanujan quotes a twelfth-century Sanskrit poem from Kshemendra's *Kavikanthabharana,* entitled "What a Poet Should Know" :

> ...he should go
> among many people
> in many places
> and learn their languages. (*CE* : 123)

and recommends it as "almost a recipe for world literature." This overtly shows that Ramanujan's poetics is deeply rooted in Indian poetic traditions. The poets of Indian Diaspora quite often express their annoyance at the controversies over re-located homelands. Uma Parameswaran gives vent to her exasperation in these words :

> ...editors and anthologies conspire to promote the perception that there are permanent disjuinctions between the old and new homelands; a stereotyping of old as good, new as negative, or the other extreme that old is destitution and oppression, the new plerity and freedom; granted that often our sweetest songs are those that tell of saddest thought; I wish anthologists would include a variety of moods and messages instead of harping on the same chord (Parameswaran).

Pondering over the peculiarities of the inmates and the items of the Indian cultural-syndrome in his well-known poem "Small-Scale Reflections on a Great House," Ramanujan is struck by several oddities, "And also, anything that goes out/will come back, processed..." (*CP* : 97). This processing engages the poet's attention in "Waterfalls in a Bank," a poem of stock-taking, a personal balance sheet :

> As I transact with the past as with another
> country with its own customs, currency,
> stock-exchange, always
> at a loss when I count my change :... (*CP* : 189)

Ramazani perceptively reads "at a loss" punningly since cultural interaction is a mutual process and this proposition need not be treated in terms of personal loss or gain for the one participant or the other. However, his elaboration of change in Ramanujan's case as "comically diminished version of the family and culture from which he came" (Ramazani : 48) can be contested. Ramazani appears to look upon this trait as the poet's weakness, inevitably damaging to his creative output. If someone is bent upon regarding him a 'diminished version,' he is also an enriched rendering of his inherited faith. It would be in the fitness of things to gloss over what Ramanujan considers as the end-result of such exchanges which "lead to definition, redefinition, a dialogue with the other where each returns to himself, reflected, refracted, even alienated and thereby redefined" (Ramanujan, 1982 : 142).

This exhaustive discussion of three early Ramanujan poems which initiate some of his major creative pre-occupations of later years identifies a serious inaccuracy in the existing Ramanujan scholarship. It is tempting to read his other early Indian poems also to set the critical perspective right in respect of this major Indian poet in English.

WORKS CITED

Chellappan, K. and Kanaka Bhashyam. 1984. "Encounter and Synthesis in the Poetry of A.K. Ramanujan." *Journal of Indian Writing in English.* 12, 2 (July) : 96-104.

Desai, S.K. 1984. "Mixing Memory and Desire : Small-Scale Reflections on the Poetry of A.K. Ramanujan" in M.K. Naik, (ed.) *Perspectives on Indian Poetry in English.* New Delhi : Abhinav : 109-23.

Devy, G.N. 1981. "Alienation as Means of Self-Exploration : A Study of A.K. Ramanujan's Poetry." *Chandrabhaga*, 6 (Winter), 5-19.

Dulai, Surjit S. 1989. "First and Only Sight." *Journal of South Asian Literature,* 24, 2 : 149-75.

King, Bruce. 1993. An Undated Communication to the author.

Kulshrestha, Chirantan. 1980. "The Self in A.K. Ramanujan's Poetry" in his (ed.) *Contemporary Indian English Verse : An Evaluation.* New Delhi : Arnold Heinemann : 175-86.

Parameswaran, Uma. 1997. Communication to the author dated 14 July.

Parthasarathy, R. 1976 (ed.) *Ten Twentieth-Century Indian Poets.* New Delhi : Oxford Univ. Press.

Patke, Rajeev S. 1995. "Ithacan Voyages : The Poetry of R. Parthasarathy and A.K. Ramanujan" in C.R. Yaravintelimath *et al.* (eds.) *New*

Perspectives in Indian English Literature. New Delhi : Sterling : 112-26.

Rao, K.R. 1997. "A.K. Ramanujan and the Poetics of Order." *Literary Half-Yearly*, 38, 2 (July) : 102-06.

Rao, P. Mallikarjuna. 1996. "The Poetry of Exile : A Study of A.K. Ramanujan" in M.K. Bhatnagar. (ed.) *Indian Writings in English*, Vol. 1. New Delhi : Atlantic : 59-67.

Ramanujan, A.K. 1980. "Between Two Worlds" (An interview by Rama Jha), *Times of India*, 20 Jan. : III.

———1999. *The Collected Essays of A.K. Ramanujan*, Vinay Dharwadker (ed.). New Delhi : Oxford Univ. Press. Referred to as *CE*.

———1995. *The Collected Poems of A.K. Ramanujan*. Vinay Dharwadker (ed.). New Delhi : Oxford Univ. Press. Referred to as *CP*

———1982. "Parables and Commonplaces" in Guy Amirthanayagam (ed.). *Writers in East-West Encounter : New Cultural Bearings*. London : Macmillan ; 138-49.

———1990-91. "Stranger." *Poetry Review*, 80, 4 : 38.

Ramazani, Jahan. 1998. "Metaphor and Postcoloniality : The Poetry of A.K. Ramanujan" *Contemporary Literature*, 39, 1 (Spring) : 27-53.

Sengupta, S. 1992. "Quest for Identity or Reappraisal? A Second Look at Ramanujan's Poetry" in R.S. Pathak (ed.) *Quest for Identity in Indian English Writing*; Vol. II. New Delhi : Bahri : 82-94.

Sharma, N.L. 1994. "Impact of American Milieu and Quest for Reality in A.K. Ramanujan's Poetry" in Suman Bala (ed.) *American Literature Today*. New Delhi : Prestige : 181-88.

3

The Points of Return : Poetry of A.K. Ramanujan

—NIRANJAN MOHANTY

Introduction

"The poems are metaphysical," writes Krittika M. Ramanujan in the "Preface" to A.K. Ramanujan's *Collected Poems,* referring to *The Black Hen* Poems, "and full of a frightening darkness. There is a sense of both a pressure towards this darkness and a simultaneous revulsion from it. The poems begin to seem denser and fuller than anything the poet had done before, the culmination of forty-seven years of writing poetry. It is almost impossible to avoid the idea that the poems seem to press towards death and disintegration and even beyond to transmutation, like lines drawn from different angles which converge on a single point, without apparent intention, and yet inevitably" (*CP* : 15). This paper is an attempt to critically examine the aesthetic configurations of the points of return in the poetry of A.K. Ramanujan.

It also tries to show how these points of return finally get converged at one point which inevitably serves to uphold and celebrate Ramanujan's poetic vision, aesthetically oriented and moulded conscientiously by a strong historical sense.

These points of return constitute an imaginary hinter-land supported and sharpened by memory. Like every expatriate writer or poet, Ramanujan maps out his points of return, partly to find out a redress for his problem of identity, partly to salvage the problems involved in his creative pursuit, partly to transcend the burdens of reality, partly to whet his awareness of the present not as a mere extension of the past, but as a moment in the cyclical order of time and history; and perhaps, partly to authenticate a maturity and perfection in terms of his creative vision.

Ramanujan's points of return are history — personal, social or cultural and linguistic — home or family, myth, and the self. The return to a point is perpetuated from a point in the present, without making the process an exhibition of a sentimental or nostalgic association. The poet is fully aware that such a return is inevitable, inescapable. But the return is being ordained by a kind of detachment that the creative medium has granted, that the physical absence (from such points) has generated. It is interesting further to notice in Ramanujan's poetry that the return to particular point involves, a diffusion of all other points, initiating a syncretic process which gets aptly appropriated by the labyrinthine structure of the poem. This, to my mind, is a signalling achievement. Perhaps, such an absorbing process has been mastered by Ramanujan through his translation of classical Tamil and Kannada poems. Krittika Ramanujan writes differently to suggest such a process :

> "Animals appear every where in the poems, but the poems are not "about" animals. They have a double vision. The poems are about life, death, cycles of birth, pain and love. They are also about poetry. They are full of irony, humour, paradox and sudden reversals" (*CP* : 16).

Molly Daniels Ramanujan in her "A Note on The Black Hen and After" also hints at the same aspect when she writes :

> "Ever the Keatsian chameleon, in the final sixth of his life Ramanujan could forge contraries to recreate a world in which he could, like his salamanders, find birth in death and death in birth. He prayed for double vision and found it in the interconnectedness of vegetable and mineral, man and animal. Above all, he found life-in-art and art-in-life" (*CP* : 278-79).

Vinay Dharwadker in his "Introduction" makes an interesting observation with regard to the types of poems that Ramanujan wrote. He discovers five "concentric circles" "in which the outermost periphery contains representations of various environments that lie on the edge of the poet's experience, while the innermost periphery brings together poems about the things that are closest to him" (*CP* : 30-31). Dharwadker maintains that the poet's self constitutes the fifth circle :

> "In the fifth and smallest circle, which is compressed almost to a point, we come face to face with the poet by himself, as the individual who experiences everything, comforts himself more closely than anything else, and serves as the subjective centre which gives all the concentric zones of experience their basic structure and meaning" (*CP* : 31).

Thus, Dharwadker's observation can be illustrated through a picture like this :

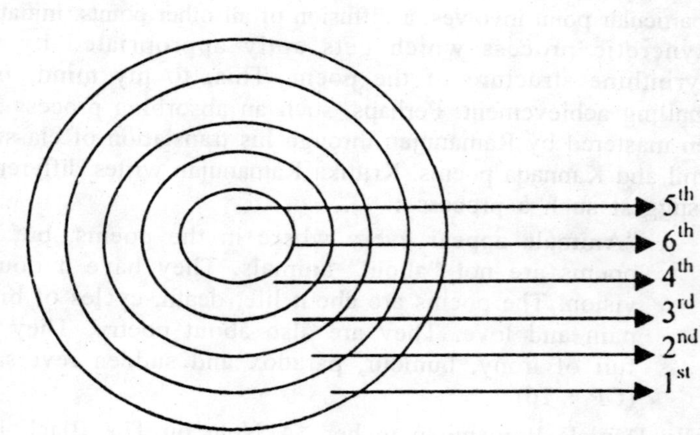

Picture : One

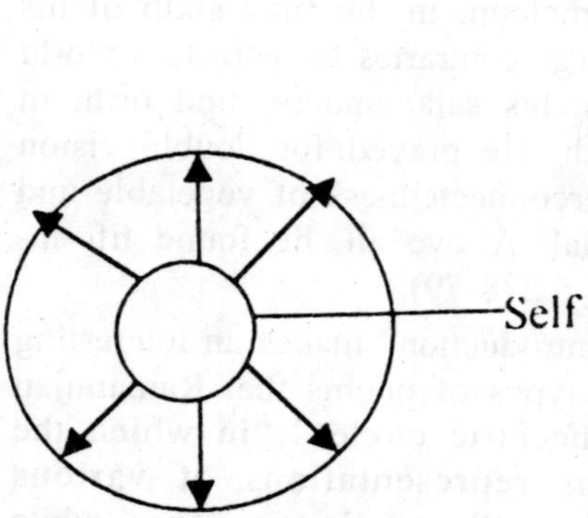

Picture : Two

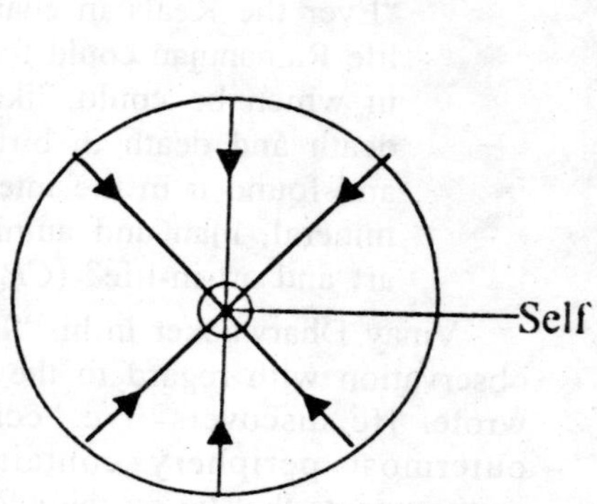

Picture : Three

What I propose to suggest is that Ramanujan's poetry, both in terms of the creative process and its structure can be presented through other picture.

The Self occupies a central position in the circle of creative consciousness so as to have a total and human point of view both of the self and of the world beyond the self. The self from the centre retains a tendency to move towards the periphery. Therefore, the self is punctuated by a centrifugal force to relate itself to different point outside the self (pict. 1). In picture no. 2, it has been shown how the self comes out of the centre and circumnavigates all points outside the self, establishing a circular connection and then the self from the points on the periphery moves back to its original position. Ramanujan's poems, contain a tensional quality because of their dichotomous conflict in terms of attempting to achieve objectivity and subjectivity. The tensional quality is acquired by the poems because of the centrifugal and centripetal movements of the self. The expansion and the contraction of the self, in a way, defines the indeterminacy of the self — as though it were a double-eyed water bug, "weightless/on the ripple skin" (*CP* : 3) of a poem. Such a self is fully aware of its tiny ironies and paradoxes which govern its movements from and to. It is fully aware that "Touch alone has untouchable" or "even near is too for" (*CP* : 77). The poetic vision emanating from such a self can only become ironic. Vinay Dharwadker observes :

> "In his poetry, this integrity injects a unique urgency into his negotiations between body and mind, nature and culture, and history and contemporaneity. It also results in the constant, unpredictable movement of his poems in which structure articulates content, but connection thrives on disconnection; nature contains the body, but the body also contains nature; and the microcosm mirrors the macrocosm, but the whole finds its truest form in the fragment. Like his final vision of love, war and death, in 'Bosnia,' his essential, life-long ideal of integrity could only be ironic" (*CP* : 38).

The points of return as well as the nature of return as ensconsed in the poetry of Ramanujan, have obviously been governed and punctuated by and integrated to the poet's ironic vision.

Return to home and/or Family

Home or family is central to Ramanujan's creative consciousness, both as a social or cultural unit or institution and as a concept or idea. The self at the centre inheres a tendency to relate itself to or offer a movement to the point on the periphery, representing home or family. Such a return decisively resolves the poet's problem of identity, sanctions a kind of security, orchestrates a kind of solace for not being altogether faceless, illustrates a type of rootedness or relatedness, weaves an experiential web which is authentic. But the resolution, to my mind, is tentative, tangentially purposeful. The return only takes place at the level of imagination. However, the impossibility of a corporal displacement (from the U.S. to South India) because of Ramanujan's American citizenship and finally because of his death in Chicago, would obviate the tentativeness of his return, and acclimatize the ironic stance. Ramanujan's physical return to India, might not have resulted in the kind of poetry that he has written by encapsulating the unalleviated tensional quality, which with its sureness of touch and intensity has become the embodiment of a gifted rarity and richness.

In one of the early poems "Snakes," one can trace out the movements of the self. The subjective self catalogues the moments or situations when he is reminded of the snakes. The second stanza of the poem is all about the ways in which the snakes move, the detailed physical description of the snakes, with only a tangential reference to some "terrible aunt." The vagueness, alienness of the aunt gets displaced by the image of the mother who "gives them milk/in saucers. She watches them suck/and bare the black-line design/etched on the brass of the saucer" (*CP* : 4). The mild irony on the snakeman whose only concern is the "smiling money" of the poet's father, is interesting. The self then touches upon the image of the sister whose "knee-long braid has scales" (*CP* : 5). The poem gets concluded with the image of the subjective self that can walk through the wood without fear or panic.

In "A Wobbly Top" Ramanujan tries to capture the dynamic, sustaining relationship between the father and the son. The wobbly top — a gift from the father — is dear to the son. This gift, retains, scars within which are not visible, because of the top's fast rotation. The top, therefore, stands for the memory of the father. Like the top, the memory of the father moves within the poet so fast that it appears still, it does away with its scars. The top as a gift illustrates the vastness of the relationship that exists between the father and the son. Thus the poem begins with the image of the father, but gets concluded with the vastness of a relationship to which the son is exposed.

Similarly the poem "Of Mothers, among other things" begins with the poet's self that relates itself to the mother's "twisted black bone tree" (*CP* : 61), and ends with the image of the self that licks bark in the mouth after observing the sensible fingers picking up grain of rice from the "kitchen floor" (*CP* : 61).

In "Love Poem for Wife 1" and "Love Poem for Wife 2" Ramanujan illustrates the ambivalent nature of his own self, the self of the wife and of the relationship between these two selves of the husband and wife. The 'Poem 1' begins with the difference between the husband and wife, through the image of the unshared childhood, and progresses through patterning of differences. He tries to bring about a hypothetical solution to this problem of ambivalence. The solution has been casually, tentatively presented, so that the irony used retains a double edge, first at his own self and then at the superstition-ridden practice of the childhood marriage in the Hindu families.

> Or we should do as well-meaning
> hindus did,
> betroth us before birth,
> forestalling separate horoscopes
> and mothers' first period,
> and wed us in the oral cradle
> and carry marriage back into
> the namelessness of childhoods. (*CP* : 67)

The poet's subtle irony reveals that there is the possibility of sharing childhood in child-marriage, but that does not ensure harmony of relationship between husband and wife in later years. Similarly in 'Poem 2' the poet shows the difference between himself and his wife who wears always a 'changing syriac face.' In spite of her anger, the poet has no hesitation to lose his face in her to become 'androgynous as a god' (*CP* : 84), and to become happy. Ramanujan, in the course of reflecting the diverse strands of his relationship, touches on other individuals of the family, and on social rituals and institutions too. The self comes, out of the centre but circuits to relate itself to other points, and finally returns to its original position at the centre where he seeks to resolve the problems experienced while circuiting through the other points on the periphery. Ramanujan employs similar strategies in "Any Cow's Horn can Do it," "History," "Obituary," "Elements of Composition," "Ecology," "Death and the Good Citizen," "Son to Father to Son," "Drafts," "Extended Family," "Love Poem for a Wife and Her Trees," "Looking for the Centre" and "Death in Search of a Comfortable Metaphor."

The cold ironic reportorial tone in "Small-scale Reflections on a Great House' reveals the strange captivating powers of a house, that houses in a joint family. The dialectical nature of the house of which the poet-reporter is an inseparable part, amply proves the poet's relationship with the house. The house has been given a personality as though it were a member of the family whose merit lies in its utter sense of possessiveness. To my mind, it seems that Ramanujan makes use of a prophecy as he begins the poem :

> Sometimes I think that nothing
> That ever comes into the house
> Goes out. (*CP* : 96)

Even if the body of Ramanujan has gone out of this house, the spirit of the self never has gone out. Indirectly, by depicting the possessive nature of the house, the poet is alluding to his own inability to dispossess the house.

In 'History' Ramanujan in his characteristic reportorial, unbiased manner brings to focus the selfishness of the 'petite little aunt' and two of great-aunt's daughters, one dark one fair, who 'alternately, picked up their mother's body clean... all except the gold/in her teeth and the silver g-string.' For the poet, the concept of history has undergone a sea-change and it is no longer grand and romantic. For the self, family's rituals constitute history and shape the concept of history that is grounded in the selfishness of the members of the family. The self of the poet depicts almost every member of the family but remains unaffected by the incident, without failing to record the change in the little aunt's expression.

In 'Obituary' the poet presents a very much realistic picture of his father who had no control over his Brahminical birth and over his death in the fruit-market because of heart attack. The way in which the death of his father is depicted amounts to charging the dead father of the liabilities, such as 'debts' and 'daughters' and a house that 'leaned' on a 'bent coconut tree,' he left behind. But soon this charge is transformed into an affectionate, less sentimentalized allegiance due to the father who left behind "a changed mother" and more "than one annual ritual." Getting a few obituary lines in a daily published from Madras is a signalling achievement, but this achievement is deflated by matter-of-factly attitude of the consumer market where the street hawkers sell newspapers to the grocers who prepare cones with which they wrap salt, coriander and jaggery for the buyers. The consumer-market never values individual emotions and sentiments. Such emotions remain dear to the ones who have been affected by the death or absence of the father. The poet comes back to the centre of his own self to perpetuate the legacy of rituals in the absence of the father. I am at once reminded of what V.S. Naipaul writes in his *The Enigma of Arrival* :

> "We were immemorially people of the country side, far from the courts of princes, living according to rituals we didn't always understand and yet were unwilling to dishonor because that would cut us off from the past, the sacred earth, the gods" (Naipaul : 351).

In "Elements of Composition," what remains striking is Ramanujan's capacity for absorption. The self at the centre critically examines, explores its possible dimension to identify its true nature. By way of cataloguing and juxtaposing two distinct levels of the self — one diasporic and the other native — Ramanujan harps on the kind of amalgamation that has gone into the making of his personality. He once admitted :

> "English and my disciplines (Linguistics, Anthropology) give me my 'outer' forms — linguistic, metrical, logical and other such way of shaping experience; and my thirty years in India, my frequent visits and field trips, my personal and professional preoccupations with Kannada, Tamil, the classics and folklore give me my substance, my 'inner' forms, images and symbols. They are continuous with each other, and I no longer can tell what comes from where" (Parthasarathy : 96).

What an honest acknowledgement of the assimilation and absorption of the two cultures — one, eastern and the other western or basically American — within the self. This results in the formation of a self of the poet which acquires a distinctive identity. Ramanujan's poems are inevitably the product of this distinctive identity so that the poet convincingly declares :

I pass through them
as they pass through me (*CP* : 122)

Or

I lose, decompose
into my elements,
into other names and forms,
past, and passing, tenses
without times,
caterpillar on a leaf, eating,
being eaten. (*CP* : 123)

This poem "Elements of Composition" therefore sums up the essence of the poetic self, and resolves the problems of a dichotomous identity which apparently traverses through the woods of his poetry.

In "Death and the Good Citizen" Ramanujan cherishes a hope to die in his own native land, for in a culture not his own, 'his tissue will never graft,' and he can never be compost for jasmine, eggplant. He prefers to be cremated in Sanskrit and sandalwood, and to be "sterilized to a scatter of ash" (*CP* :

136). The poet's inner forms never intend to dispossess their ties with the native land. Affirmation of such an attitude, in terms of his explicit preference, makes Ramanujan an instinctive insider, a settler in the blood.

In "Extended Famıly," the poet while juxtaposing the sets of value-posited objects, maps out the inevitability of his return from the peripheral perambulation to the centre of his self which is rooted in his own native culture. Even if he 'bathes' like his grandfather, he is deprived of the sanctimony of the bath in the 'dry chlorine water' in the absence of the Ganges water. He slaps soap on his back like his father, but dries himself with an 'unwashed towel.' Like his mother he listens to the morning songs — but these are faint in Japanese. Towards the fag end of Ramanujan's creative career, as his poems attest, he seems to have been haunted by the images of his mother and father. The element of nostalgia takes him back to the days when he left for the U.S. In a small poem "Farewell" he whirls back to the fond memory of his mother :

> Mother's farewell had no words,
> no tears, only a long look
> that moved on your body
> from top to toe.
> with the advice that you should
> not forget your oil bath
> every Tuesday
> when you go to America. (*CP* : 259)

He is concerned about these images and like a child he innocently tries to know where exactly they go, the images such as :

> cutting across the bangles broken
> on mother's hour of widowhood, things taken
> for lost like Father and his unspoken dying
> thought in the fruit market in '53. (*CP* : 271)

Perhaps Ramanujan through these images makes an attempt to renew himself, revisit himself in order to do away with his present state of helplessness in the absence of such fond images.

What Ramanujan tangentially hints at, rather sardonically, is that he catalogues the likeness of his actions with his family members, such as Grandfather, Father and Mother, but seems to have been dismayed by the discovery of his own shallowness, artificiality in contrast to their sanctimony. And the poem gets concluded with a peculiar plight of the self that has to depend "on several/people/yet/to come" (*CP* : 170) for his future. Both his past and future are dependent on many others. It is primarily because of the recognition of this dependence that the self does not risk losing its face "in a world without places" (*CP* : 166). This poem, therefore, fully subscribes to the model that this paper has attempted to prescribe. In other words, the self leaves its central position, moves to periphery to establish its connection with other points, and comes back to the original position at the centre, acquiring the wisdom of self-discovery. This process of self-discovery does not, however, romanticize the 'other' outside the self nor does it romanticize the self. To my mind, the discovery of such a process is because of the influences entailed by, what Ramanujan calls the 'outer forms.' The nature of self that one encounters in Ramanujan's poetry at once brings to my mind what Fanon states :

> "The consciousness of self is not closing of a door to communication. Philosophic thought teaches us, on the contrary, that it is its guarantee. National consciousness, which is not nationalism, is the only thing that will give us an international dimension" (Fanon : 199).

The self in Ramanujan is not an enclosed entity. It retains its freedom to transact with other points beyond the self — the points such as family, society, culture, religion, institution of marriage, — without any prejudice, or bias, or exoticist euphoria which exerts a smoothness and ease to transaction. This is why possibly Ramanujan's poetry remains so distinctive and original, mapping out a vision that enshrines the direction that Indian poetry in English is likely to take so as to legitimize its authenticity, originality and global acceptability.

Return to Religion and Myth

A person's identity is unique and very much a private thing. But this identity takes a complete shape because it develops from and within a specific culture. It is, therefore, essentially determined by and related to social and historical factors. This specificity of a cultural identity often urges on to the development of a recalcitrant personality which consciously or unconsciously tries to retain its essential self, in spite of physical displacement or what in the diasporic discourse is known as migrancy. In case of Ramanujan, the development of a recalcitrant personality seems to have been inhibited by his absorption to what Ramanujan calls the "outer" forms. Ramanujan's poetry should be read and located, what Richard W. Noland (Noland : 100) in another context suggests, first within the context of author's present stage in the human life cycle. Thus the primacy of the present stage over all other stages of development of the self in the past would always render an objectivity, which otherwise would have been impossible to achieve.

Ramanujan's Hindu poems — "A Hindu to his body," "The Hindoo : he reads his GITA and is calm at all events" and "The HINDOO — the only risk" — unravel a deep ironic stance. The irony is explicit even in the use of 'oo' instead of 'u' in the word Hindu. Descending from an orthodox Brahmin family, and being a Hindu himself, Ramanujan is sceptical about the god-fearing Hindu attitude, which insulates him with a selfishness that he never reveals to others for that would amount to debasing, demeaning the religion itself. What Ramanujan hints at is the dual nature of the self — one real and hidden and secretive, the other apparent, pretentious, tentative and false. The three poems try to show the gap between the real and the apparent. The real self remains hidden behind the veil of the religion. What the body does to a Hindu or what he signifies in the body being a Hindu, has been catalogued by Ramanujan, the mode of cataloguing in itself is expository of an ironic intent :

> Gave me fingers to clutch
> at grace, at malice; and ruffle
> someone else's hair; to fold a man's
> shadow back on his world;
> to hold in the dark of the eye
> through a winter and a fear
> the poise, the shape of a breast;
> a pear's silence, in the calyx
> and the noise of a childish fist. (*CP* : 40)

The same Hindu who is so much attached to the body, also intends to "rise in the sap of tress" so as to "feel the weight/ of honey-hives" and "the burlap weave of weaver-birds" in his hair (*CP* : 40).

The second Hindu poem, in the Petrarchan sonnet form without its regular, rhyme scheme, is a superb case of irony. The secred scripture of the Hindus, the Gita, teaches one to have control over one's senses. It teaches one to be more human and compassionate. It brings one closer to calmness. It does not make one non-chalant to human suffering and misery. The personae in this poem has read the Gita, but has lost the spirit of its wisdom :

> 'I do not marvel
> when I see good and evil :
> I just walk
> over the iridescence
> of horsepiss after rain. Knives, bombs, scandal,
> and cowdung fall on women in wedding lace :
> I say nothing, I take care not to gloat. (*CP* : 79)

The personae has no envy in watching lovers kiss, but he cannot afford to miss it. He also looks at wounds 'calmly,' when the wound demands care and sympathy. The concluding image lets loose the ironic intent :

> Yet when I meet on a little boy's face
> the prehistoric yellow eyes of a goat
> I choke, for ancient hands are at my throat. (*CP* : 79)

Ramanujan's satire is not drawn towards Hinduism or the sacred scripture, but against those Hindus who read or know the contents of the scripture and miss its spirit. Ramanujan through these poems tries to ascertain that half-knowledge would never make an individual wise; and that one must not follow the the Gita by its letter but by its essence and spirit. Ramanujan's dig at some Hindus is reiterated in his "The Hindu : the only risk." The Hindu whose knowledge about his self and the world is incomplete, biased and selfish, has been made the victim of Ramanujan's whetted irony. The personae, who is well-versed in the Gita, and who is likely to retain his calm and composed self, feels it a risk to retain his calm and heart's simple beat at neighbour's striptease or a 'friend's suicide.' He also does not take the risk of handling kitchen knife, for he may be tempted to maim himself or his wife or the child for this or that. But he never takes any risk in terms of losing or getting "three square meals" a day. His interest lies in every thing, even in the 'dead street-dog.' He wants to involve himself in every thing but he is afraid of death : for, he does not want "to be caught at sea, battle, riot, adultery or hate" (*CP* : 90). What the poet exposes is the persona's selfishness and 'heartlessness.'

A similar dig at the tentativeness of religious temper is illustrated in "Entries for a Catalogue of Fears," in which the persona makes promises to be "charitable one day" (*CP* : 87). At sixty only he has started talking "now and then of God," and not earlier. His talk of God stems only from his fear of death because he is already sixty. He is willing to find "reasons to be fair/every where/to the even and to the odd" and

> see karma
> in the fall of a tubercular sparrow,
> in the newspaper deaths in Burma
> of seventy-one men, women and children,
> actually see the one in the Many,
> losing a lifetime of double vision
> with one small adjustment
> of glasses. (*CP* : 87)

Ramanujan's ironic mode achieves its height in "Prayers to Lord Murugan." Lord Murugan is the "ancient Dravidian god of fertility, joy, youth, beauty, war and love. He is represented as a six-faced god with twelve hands" (*CP* : 113). The poet laments over the present mode of prayers. He laments over the loss of ancient ritualistic practices at the altar of Lord Murugan. This anxiety and concern over the plight of the Lord reminds at once of Keats' concern for Psyche in "Ode to Psyche."

The timely obviousness of Ramanujan's dig at the modern man's sudden withdrawal from the spiritual centre is really fascinating. His regret over the loss of faith is explicit very much in the opening section :

> O where are the cockscombs and where

the beaks glinting with new knives
at crossroads

when will orange banners burn
among blue trumpet flowers and the shade
of tree

waiting for lightnings? (*CP* : 113)

The lightning is no longer accepted as a divine revelation. The sacrificial altar of Lord is dry and bereft of animation. The prayer is no longer an instrument of human good. It has lost its devotional content. It is devoid of sincerity. It is no longer a hymn of the heart. Its canvas has been utterly reduced to manifest individual selfishness. Ramanujan rightly highlights this incurable degeneration when he writes :

Lord of headlines,
help us read
the small print.
Lord of the sixth sense,
give us back
our five sense. (*CP* : 116)

* * *

Lord of lost travellers,
find us. Hunt us
down.
Lord of answers
cure us at once
of prayers. (*CP* : 117)

Prayer, which is redemptive, has become a disease and an instrument of uneasiness. That is why the modern man, divorced from the spiritual centre, from the centre of faith can articulate such prayers to get rid of them. Living in such a world of vacancy, emptiness and corruption or infection, the poet interrogates his own sense of helplessness in "Questions" :

my head's soft crown bathed in mother's blood,
wearing tatters of attachments, bursting
into the cruelties,
of earthly light, infected air? (*CP* : 130)

In "Pleasure" Ramanujan's characteristic irony holds a Jaina monk its captive. This particular monk because of long celibacy is caught by 'spring fever' so that his interest in 'mango blossom,' 'petal,' 'stamen' and butterfly becomes increasingly violent which leads his "several mouths" to :

thirsting for breast,
buttock, smells of finger,
long hair, short hair,
the wet of places never dry,
skin roused even by
whips, self touching self,
all philosophy slimed by its own saliva,
cool Ganges turning,
sensual on him. (*CP* : 139)

The great monk who intended to derive pleasure in pain — the philosophy of Jainism — is now given to pleasure only. One who considered trampling on the ants as sinful does not hesitate to stand on the ant-hill of "red fire ants." But soon the ants transform his philosophy of pleasure and pleasure-in-pain into pain only for "the ants climb/tattooing/him, limb by limb,/and covet his body." In "Waterfalls in a Bank" Ramanujan exposes the vulgarity of a paralytic sadhu who "lifts with his one good finger/his loincloth, and pisses standing/like a horse — aiming his stream/at two red flowers on the oleander bush" (*CP* : 190). In "At Zero" the poet depicts another saint — a "potter-saint" who buries his "youngest child alive" and dances to please his god (*CP* : 201).

In yet another poem "The Guru" which obviously reminds me of Ezekiel's "Guru," Ramanujan criticizes the unholy nature of the guru. A 'guru' is supposed to be wise, and a guide for others. He is supposed to love all, without making any discrimination of gender or race, rich or poor. But the 'guru' that Ramanujan limns flouts all norms of wisdom, for he advises :

Forgive the weasel his tooth
forgive the tiger his claw but
do not forgive the woman

her malice or the man his envy

* * *

do not give woman her freedom
nor man his midday meal till he begs. (*CP* : 251)

And funniest part of the guru is that he commands the persona to polish his shoe. The guru is full of invective, full of hunger for power, full of anger. If this is what a guru is, the hope for guiding mankind is lost for ever. Obviously, Ramanujan's dig is not at all gurus, but at a few selfish ones, and the false ones. The poet by his subtle use of irony brings to focus the falsehood that the guru embodies.

From the examination of the poems involving religion, it is evident that Ramanujan, whose origin lies in the South Indian Brahmin family, as a creative artist can hardly afford to remain silent on those aspects of religion which have experienced a steady degeneration. His ironic stance should not be adjudged as an invective against Hinduism. As a creative writer he has every right to debunk the follies and foibles which lie deeply within the matrix of religion, or society or culture at large. Ramanujan's detachment, his sense of ease in objectively viewing the world outside the self, possibly stems from and is because of the amalgamation of the 'outer' and 'inner' forms — the one nurturing and influencing the other, the one augmenting the supporting the other, without a verifiably inhibiting bias. This to my belief is a signalling achievement. Precisely because of this attitude, Ramanujan's ironic mode assumes a sophistication and sharpness, rare in Indian poetry in English.

In some poems Ramanujan makes use of myths, legends, tales from epic — mostly Indian — not only to endorse and affirm his instinctive access to the rich cultural heritage of his native and, but also to ascertain their contemporary relevance. In spite of material progress, scientific inventions, myths remain central to a culture. By revoking myths in his poetry, Ramanujan tries to perpetuate the link between the past and the present. In myths the poet discovers the continuity of his own self, in so far as they offer an intuitive awareness of the reality, in the present. But in case of Ramanujan, the myths often act as background to sharpen the edges of his irony.

"A Minor Sacrifice" begins with a familiar tale from the epic, and is followed by an incident chosen from day-to-day life. Both the tales in the narrative are conclusive, and independent of each other. But Ramanujan establishes a connection, harping on the perpetual tension between the scientific temper, and god-fearing, Karma-adhering attitude. The poem does not resolve the tension, but the manner in which the poem comes to an end suggests that killing or sacrificing insects or animals is an act of reproachful sin. The poem indicates clear cut Hindu and Buddhist influences on Ramanujan.

In the tale from the epic, a certain mischievous king kills a snake and for fun places the dead snake around a sage's neck and earns a curse of an early death by snakebite. The king's son avenged the snakes by performing a sacrifice. Magic — drawn snakes from everywhere leapt into the altar of sacrificial fire and got burnt. This mythical tale of sacrifice is followed by another narrative in which a certain uncle kills a scorpion and shows its poison head to Shivanna and Gopu — the children at once become interested in riding the world of scorpions by witch craft. They have to appease the 'twelve-handed god of scorpions' by offering "one thousand live grasshoppers caught in a new moon Tuesday" (*CP* : 146). The children, accordingly, steal three pickle jars on a new moon Tuesday. By evening they could collect only ninety nine. Gopu keeps the jars under his bed and dreams of punishment in the Hindu hell. On Wednesday morning, the mother of Shivanna informs everyone that he has been admitted to the hospital because of "some strange twitching disease" (*CP* : 148). Shivanna dies of that disease, and the uncle who was instrumental to provoking the children coldly makes self-explanatory interrogation :

> Did you know that Shivanna,
> he clawed and kicked the air
> all that day, that new moon Tuesday,
> like some bug on its back? (*CP* : 148)

Ramanujan finds no fault with the "Savage innocent"

(*CP* : 148) the children. His dig is at the matured uncle who is responsible for Shivanna's death.

Ramanujan's mythology poems — Mythologies I, II and III — are slightly different from "A Minor Sacrifice," in terms of the use of irony in degrees. In the first two poems Ramanujan juxtaposes the reality of the myth with the fact of his real self. In both these poems he tries to capture myth/a thing of the past — to show the continuity of his own self from the past to the present. He also incorporates into these poems a prayer motif, like a true Hindu at the fag end of his life. Not only the sense of death, and not the fear of the death, is evident, but also a willingness to be united with the divine is very much implicit in the prayer motif.

In "Mythologies I," Krishna and Putana myth is revoked. Kansa, the notorious king and uncle of Krishna, sends Putana to feed baby Krishna from her poison-coated nipple to kill him. But the divine baby could envision the heinous conspiracy and brought an end to her life. The poet's exacting depiction, even if precise, is remarkable :

> The child took her breast
> in his mouth and sucked it right out of her chest.
> Her carcass stretched from north to south.
> She changed, undone by grace,
> from deadly mother to happy demon,
> found life in death. (*CP* : 221)

To be killed by god is to realize salvation. So the demon is at once "happy" to be dead to experience a new life, purged off all demonic qualities. The poet's prayer is, therefore, significant. This life has infused all poison into the poet's self. He is willing to be resurrected, to begin a new life, ensconced in salvation. This is the most honest and sincere prayer which for every Hindu is prayable :

> O Terror with a baby face,
> suck me dry. Drink my venom.
> Renew my breath. (*CP* : 221)

In the second poem, the poet revokes the myth of the Lord Vishnu who tarnished the tyrannical king Hiranya Kashyapu, the atheist father of Prahlad, the devotee of Lord Vishnu. Lord Vishnu, in order to prove his omnipresence and to protect his devotee and his faith, appeared from the concrete pillar of the palace, in a half-man-half-lion shape and tore off the king, keeping him on his knees at the threshold. The myth is followed by the poet's honest prayer :

> connoisseur of negatives and assassin
> of certitudes, slay now my faith in doubt.
> End my commerce with bat and night
> owl. Adjust my single eye, rainbow bubble,
> so I too may see all things double. (*CP* : 226)

The poet's prayer to enable him to have a 'double vision' and to do away with his 'doubt' epitomizes his faith in Vishnu and alludes to his maturing vision with which he can see the inner and the outer side of things real. By juxtaposition of the mythical with the real, the poet's assertion of their interdependence reinvigorates his faith wherein lie his roots.

In "Mythologies 3" the poet dramatizes a situation in which the wife warns her husband to keep himself off from her at the time of worshipping Shiva. She also advises him not to touch her thrice for that would amount to losing her for ever. The husband could never believe her, for his only interest lies in her body :

> And all he could think of was her round breast,
> her musk, her darling navel and the rest. (*CP* : 228)

When the wife utters "Om, Om," and is devotionally offering her prayers to Lord Shiva, the husband, who is selfish, who does not understand what devotion could mean, is busy in touching her. Her ritualistic gesture was misconstrued by the husband as her willingness to be engaged in sexual act. But, as pointed by her earlier, she is engaged in communion with Lord Shiva :

> She saw Him then, unborn, form of forms, the Rider,
> His white Bull chewing cud in her backyard (*CP* : 228).

Ramanujan simply juxtaposes two individuals to show the difference between them — the one devotional, the other physical, the one is for the spirit, the other for the body or matter. By mere juxtaposition, the poet evidences the superiority of the one over the other.

Conclusion

Ramanujan's poetry, therefore, elicits a new perspective in which both the self at the centre and points on the periphery to which the self often returns to are of equal significance particularly because of the symbiotic relationships that exist between them, that permeate through them and animate them. Privileging one over the other would amount obviously to the imbalance between Ramanujan's "inner" and "outer forms." Slowly the poet becomes aware that the centrality of the self would dissolve and what would animate the central self are these points of return :

> Letting go
> of fairy tales
> is letting go
> of what will not
> let go :
> mother, grandmother the fat cook
> in widow's white
> who fed me
> rice and ogres. (*CP* : 260)

The poet is fully aware of the transience of his self, the sureness of his mortality, for this self

> will one day be short of breath,
> lose its thrust,
> turn cold, dehydrate and leave
> a jaw bone with half a grin
> near a pond (*CP* : 209)

and it will lose its centrality. Like everyone else, he will come to dust and accept the unwritten constitution of silence:

> Everyone in this street
> will become cold, lie under stones
> or be scattered as ash in rivers and oceans (*CP* : 210)

Ramanujan is sure not only of the fierce blows of time and death, but also of what the central self has created in the form of poetry, for

> Poetry too is a tigress
> except there's no fifth
> man left on a tree

when she takes your breath
away. (*CP* : 245)

WORKS CITED

Fanon, F. 1990. *The Wretched of the Earth* (Trans) Constance Farrington. Harmondsworth : Penguin.

Naipaul, V.S. 1987. *The Enigma of Arrival.* New York : Vintage Books.

Noland, Richard W. 1973. "The Future of Psychological Criticism." *Hartford Studies in Literature,* 5 : 100.

Parthasarathy, R. (ed.). 1976. *Ten Twentieth-Century Indian Poets,* New Delhi : Oxford Univ. Press.

Ramanujan, A.K. 1995. *The Collected Poems of A.K. Ramanujan* (ed.) Vinay Dharwadker. New Delhi : Oxford Univ. Press.

4

The Fusion of the Reflective and the Introspective in A.K. Ramanujan's Poetry

—RAJALAKSHMI GOPALAN

Indo-Anglian poetry has made a significant contribution to the development of poetry in India. It has successfully voiced the multifaceted experiences of the Indian people. In this regard poets have employed varied techniques for conveying their vision of life. Indo-Anglian poetry is so complex that in order to understand an individual poet's vision of life, one has to delve deep and examine his creative perceptions with regard to the major themes of poetry like nature, love, man, heritage, myth, legend etc., on the one hand and mysticism, metaphysical longing, spirituality, philosophic concerns etc., on the other. Indo-Anglian poetry thus reflects the complexity of the Indian scenario with freshness and vitality.

Among the Indian poets writing in English, A.K. Ramanujan stands out as a unique figure for his substantial contribution to the growth and development of Indo-English poetry. An expatriate with a sense of commitment Ramanujan finds his roots in the native ethos and tradition. Though not a prolific writer, he has carved a niche for himself by combining diverse strands and themes. His inherent genius enabled him to amalgamate the critical rational outlook of the West with the rich cultural and spiritual heritage of the East. Though he had stayed for a long time in the United States, his poems strongly exhibit his warm associations with the East. In spite of his Western footing

A.K. Ramanujan has never ceased to be an Indian, which is both his asset and liability as a poet.

A.K. Ramanujan's poetry is a union of the various sights, sounds and other aspects of nature as he had perceived them and the historical, philosophic and mystical attitude with which he has responded to them. It is this synthesis of his perception of the external world with the world of his inner imaginative response which lends an extraordinary meaning to his poems. When the poet

> reflects on the world around him and registers his reactions to it in a wistful, thoughtful and photographic manner, he writes reflective poetry. On the other hand, if his [thoughts] are turned towards the internal world of memories and he is weighing the significance or insignificance of his own life, he writes introspective poetry (Gokak : 34).

A poet is an embodiment of these two different dimensions. When he stands on the threshold of the outer world and his major concern is nature, love, human heritage, he writes as a reflective poet and when he is on the way to metaphysical contemplation, spiritual illumination and visionary power, he writes as an introspective poet. Individual poets have excelled in depicting one of these worlds perfectly. But, A.K. Ramanujan's singularity lies in combining these two activities to communicate effectively the thrill and ecstasy as well as the higher level of consciousness that he has experienced in his poems.

Ramanujan's two volumes *The Striders* (1966) and *Relations* (1971) exhibit his poetic genius remarkably. His favourite themes include Indian men and women and their manners, family, relatives, life, love, death and cultural harmony. Though his production is not that huge, it has given him recognition as a poetic talent who could interpret the soul of India to the Western world. His greatness as a poet lies in his ability to poetically fuse the experiences of the outer world with the responses of the inner world. They reveal his deep obsession with the Indian ethos, psyche and its pure spirit. What is remarkable in his works is his extreme precision in combining the powerful ancient beliefs with the ironic skeptical view of actual life. His poems on insects, relatives, Hindu way of life etc., are all complicated, yet they are dealt with a sense of clarity and unmatched accuracy.

Being alienated in more than one sense, Ramanujan has employed the operational strategy of fusion "to sustain an integrated personality against a chaos of alienation" (Rao : 121). In this strategy of fusion the poet's creativity has many a time forced him to present the exotic as ordinary or the remote as immediate. The poems expose the poet's extraordinary ability to record facts in such manner that the past integrates into the present and the present into the unknown future. India's people, their customs, their cultural and spiritual heritage, their past history with its many plumes form the basis of his art. His strong associations with and firm convictions in the native culture enabled him to see the essential India despite his long stay in the United States. Poems like 'The Hindoo' : He doesn't hurt a Fly or Spider either," "The Hindoo : He reads his GITA and is calm at all events" are essentially culture specific.

Ramanujan's artistry lies in his sensitive use of language which conceals the depth of his thoughts and the deft use of themes which clarifies his vision. By skilfully employing symbols and images the poet yokes together the 'outer' and the 'inner' forms of his mind and imagination, thus adding a new colour and dimension to Indo-English poetry. Acclaimed as one of the best Indo-English poets by his contemporaries Nissim Ezekiel and R. Parthasarathy, Ramanujan employs poetry as a medium to synthesize his reflective experiences and introspective perceptions and communicate the embedded meaning. A few poems from both his collections are taken up for analysis to illustrate Ramanujan's specific purpose to use the strategy of fusion.

His first collection *The Strider* is a slim but elegant collection of poems like "The Striders," "Snakes," "Breaded Fish," "A River" etc. Superficially all these poems are precise pictures of the objects which the poet is preoccupied with. However, a close analysis reveals the synchronicity of his literary sensibilities. The title poem "The Striders" is about a particular kind of New England water bug. Its superficial description is as follows :

.................................thin ......
stemmed, bubble-eyed water bugs
See them perch
on dry capillary legs
weightless
on the ripple skin
of a stream. (*CP* : 3)

This superficial and precise description of the water bug is striking. But it is its activity in the following lines which gives an extraordinary dimension to the striders.

No, not only prophets
walk on water. This bug sits
on a landslide of lights
and drowns eye — deep
into its tiny strip
of sky. (*CP* : 3)

The ease with which the water bug exists both on land and water gives it a luminous effect bringing it almost close to a 'prophet.' Thus the poet succeeds in evoking a spiritual concreteness through the image of an ordinary amphibian.

"A River" (*CP* : 38-39) is another such poem in the same collection which reflectively draws our attention to the river 'Vaikai' which flows through Madurai, the ancient city of Tamil culture. Ramanujan's artistic secret lies in his combining the visual and the conceptual. The images created by him are basically visual but underneath these patterns of images one can discern their beauty and their modern consciousness. The poet's Indian sensibility projects the river in its two extreme stages — one when it is dry and the other when it is in spate. Such a word painting is possible only by a poet who has an eye for the minutest detail even of an ordinary phenomenon. The river in summer is just

.............a trickle
in the sand,
baring the sand ribs

where

the wet stones glistening like sleepy

crocodiles, the dry ones
shaven water-buffalos lounging in the sun.

This dryness of the river is juxtaposed with its swollenness during floods which is an exciting prospect as it induces one, to be poetic,

about only once.

In their excitement the old and the new Tamil poets "sang only of the floods" and the considerable devastation caused by the flooded river. If the early poets sang

...the way [the river] carried off three villages
one pregnant woman
and a couple of cows....

the new poets were no better as they still quoted "the old poets." The ironic tone of the poem is revealed when we deviate from the reflective level to the introspective level.

Superficially, as an evocative poem about the river, it successfully unravels the visual imagery with photographic perfection. One can perceive the contrast between the dry river and the river in floods reflectively whereas introspectively one can identify the metaphysical subtlety and artistic emotion of the poet's concern for the human suffering. What pains him is the relative attitudes of the old and the new poets and their "callousness to suffering" (Parthasarathy : 95). His human concern forces him to deride poets, who carried away by the external beauty, forget reality with "its still sad music of humanity". The spiritual and emotional sterility of the poets is conveyed when he mentions them singing only "of cities and temples" while

......no one spoke
in verse
of the pregnant woman
drowned, with perhaps twins in her
kicking at blank walls. (*CP* : 39)

Thus by integrally connecting the reflective and the introspective Ramanujan forces his readers to construct the essential meaning.

"Breaded fish" (*CP* : 7) is another significant poem in this volume where the fish in bread becomes an objective correlative to connect the persona with the past memory which is horrifying and grim. The rich subtlety with which the persona is invited to eat the bread fish is an immediate experience. The poem begins on a lighter vein :

> Specially for me, she had some breaded
> fish; even thrust a blunt-headed
> smelt into my mouth.

The persona's inability to eat the breaded fish specially made for him not only hurts the person who has prepared it but also the reader who wonders why he "could neither sit nor eat." As we read further we realize that the poet's specific use of the crystallized image of the breaded fish is to give expression to some deep rooted memory that had sunk into the persona's consciousness. This memory poem once again affirms Ramanujan's skill in mingling the present and the past and the vague and the concrete. The image of the breaded fish in the present succeeds in evoking the forgotten memory of the past where he is reminded of

> ...a dark half-naked length of a woman,
> dead on the beach in a yard of cloth, dry, rolled
> by the ebb, breaded by the grained indifference
> of sand.

One cannot but admire A.K. Ramanujan's terse use of language and the disciplined handling of imagery to evoke the hidden childhood memory which becomes disturbingly alive and leaves the persona restless.

Ramanujan's second collection *Relations* published in 1971 is a maturer collection on recollected personal experiences and emotions. The prominent feature of this collection is

> The collective nostalgia of a whole people who look back, often in an attitude of love-hate, to the past, at once drawn towards and repelled by it. The 'presence of the past' is a unique feature of the poems in this volume (Tilak : 6).

What gives artistic validity to this collection is Ramanujan's ironic stance to dramatize familiar day-to-day activities.

The most commonly read poem in this collection is "Obituary." The poem recalls and reflects on the death of his father and ironically comments on the rituals and ceremonies associated with the dead. Reflectively the poem is a remembrance of the father who is dead and gone. Its outer ironic form however does not diminish its essential introspective seriousness and poignancy. It is a kind of elegy where the poet in a mock ironic tone talks about the legacy that the poor father has left behind. But the essential concern of the poet is brought out in the poetic fusion of the personal and the impersonal. A sense of universality is achieved in linking tradition and concern. By singing the father's poverty and the mother's grief over the loss of her husband the poet affirms his real love for the departed father.

If 'Obituary' is about the father, "Of Mothers, among other things" is an impressive reflection on the mother at various stages in her life. It begins with her younger days she was like "the silk and white petal." However this pleasant reflection does not continue for a long time. Very soon the poet is introspectively drawn into grief when he expresses the changed state of his mother. In her old age there is no trace of the "silk white petal" but only

> ......her four
> still sensible fingers slowly flex
> to pick a grain of rice from the kitchen floor.
>
> (*CP* : 61)

The use of the word "still" indicates the sense of immobility and change that has come over her in her old age. But in the fusion of the reflective and the introspective we discern the poet's capacity to overcome his mother's helplessness and admire her for her will power and determination to overcome the handicap of old age.

"The Last of the Princes" (*CP* : 105) another poem in this collection, exhibits Ramanujan's sharp and acute historical sensibility. The poem combines familial experience with a historical consciousness. It is a pathetic poem on the fall of the Moghul empire, throwing light on the poverty and suffering of the royal family that falls on evil days. The poem begins from that period of history when Aurangazeb had died and the Moghul empire had lost all its glory. Its slow decay and disintegration is compared to a patient suffering from T.B. and slowly heading to a final end. One admires the poet's use of language to list the various causes that had led to the fall :

> ....this dynasty
> falling in slow motion from Aurangazeb's time;
> some of bone T.B.
> others of a London fog that went to their heads
> some of current trends, imported wine and women....

Ramanujan's poetic sensibility projects the cunning policies employed by the English to bewilder and confuse the Moghuls. He also mentions the intrigues of the English to which some members of the royal family became victims by importing wine and women.

The last of the princes who survived, a reference to Bahadur Shah Zafar, suffered from poverty and illness. However, he remained a true patriot who did not yield to the British cruelty. His pathetic suffering is portrayed by Ramanujan as follows :

> ....he lives on, to cough
> remember and sneeze, a balance of phlegm
> and bile, alternating loose bowels and hard
> sheep's pellets.

The extreme poverty to which the family is driven is touchingly depicted in the following lines :

> Two girls, Honey and Bunny, go to school
> on half fees. Wife, heir loom pearl in her nose-ring,
> pregnant again. His first son, trainee in telegraphy,
> has telegraphed thrice already for money.

By thus throwing light on individual suffering the poem actually highlights the anxiety and suffering of a people who have been for long subjected to misery and trouble.

These few chosen poems, thus illustrate Ramanujan's unique style not only to juxtapose disparate elements, but also to fuse outer forms and inner thoughts into a magnificent whole. To conclude, we can say that "Ramanujan's poetry is the expression of a poetic sensibility in which the Indian subjectivity coalesces with the Western objectivity" (Lall : 51) to establish harmony and clarity. The perennial appeal of Ramanujan's works is that, as artistic expressions they achieve a metaphysical level of creative beauty.

WORKS CITED

Gokak, V.K. (ed.). 1970. *The Golden Treasury of Indo-Anglian Poetry,* 1828-1965. New Delhi : Sahitya Akademi.

Lall, Emmannel N. 1983. *The Poetry of Encounter.* New Delhi : Sterling.

Parthasarathy, R. (ed.). 1976. *Ten Twentieth-Century Indian Poets.* New Delhi : Oxford Univ. Press.

Rao, K.R. 1979. "Reverse Romanticism : The case of A.K. Ramanujan's *The Striders*" in M.K. Naik (ed.) *Aspects of Indian Writing in English.* New Delhi : Macmillan.

Ramanujan, A.K. 1995. *The Collected Poems of A.K. Ramanujan* (ed.). Vinay Dharwadker. New Delhi : Oxford Univ. Press. Referred to as *CP* in the text.

Tilak, Raghukul. 1992. *Indian English Poets and Poetry.* New Delhi : Rama Brothers.

5

The Negotiation of Art and Life in A.K. Ramanujan's Poetry

—RAKESH N. DESAI

A.K. Ramanujan's poetry is rooted in Tamil, Indian culture and also influenced by the modern, Western creative writers. In fact, he lived for many years as an expatriate in the U.S. till the end. Self-reflexivity, a marked feature of his poetry, means here the awareness of a work of art about itself, *i.e.*, "the poem" itself as the theme of a poem. Self-reflexivity works out in two directions in Ramanujan's poetry : (1) the poems in which creative process itself is treated as a theme, (2) the poems which probe the limits of art (or poetry), a probe into the borderline between art and life. This second form of self-reflexivity is treated to its extreme by Pirandello, the Italian dramatist, in his *Six Characters in Search of an Author*. Patrick White, the Australian novelist, deals with it in *The Vivisector*. W.H. Auden in England makes it a theme of his longer poem, *The Sea and the Mirror*.

Though both the forms of self-reflexivity are coterminous, the first part of the paper focuses on the way Ramanujan's poems reflect on the creative process. Its second part concentrates on the negotiation of art and life in his poetry.

I

The title poem, "The Striders" of *The Striders* (1966) presents, as S.K. Desai observes, Ramanujan's "characteristic Imagist strategies," as he is "primarily an Imagist poet" and his poetry is "the poetry of 'seeing,' of perception" (Desai : 251). The Strider, the New England water insect, steadily hovers over the changing watery surface and defines its own reality against the varying flux of day-to-day reality. What the strider does is anticipated by the poet — the creation of an autonomous image out of the flux of life. Thus, the poem discounts life at large and closes off its poetic text : "and drowns eye-/deep/ into its tiny strip/of sky." (*CP* : 3)

Unlike "The Striders," "Which Reminds Me" takes into account the sphere of life in relation to creative process. A "measly-looking man," who suffers from minor ailments, writes "a poem" in short time, "sitting at the window of the local bus" while "going to the bank" (*CP* : 25). Though the creative act is defined within the fantastic and the realistic frontiers, the former appears to be (dis) located within the latter. So, this consequent sense of surprize, mingled with playful irony, reminds one of "the folktale tree" which makes "the mangy palace dog" pregnant while "leaving the whole royal harem/barren" (*CP* : 25). Art finds the sense of the other in life.

"On the Death of a Poem" in *Second Sight* (1986) not only continues art's encounter with the other, but also introduces a new element of terror within it. "Images" in a poem turn into "a conscience-/stricken/jury," "and come/slowly/to a sentence" (*CP* : 142). Needless to say, "sentence" means here a capital punishment as well as a grammatical unit. Moreover, the jury becomes the accused and suffers the punishment. The terms like image (the intuitive grasp of reality embodied within an image) and discourse (the rational, discursive element within a poem) as discussed by Frank Kermode in the context of symbolist historiography seem to be pertinent here (Kermode : 149-161). An intuitive Image can communicate to a reader only through the discursive sphere of sentence, the sphere of grammar and language at public level. And it is discourse which works in Auden's poems after T.S. Eliot's imagist poetry. Though the poem laments the tragic necessity of discourse for an image, it does acknowledge the presence of the other, tinged with a sense of terror.

"Drafts" (*CP* : 157-58) in the same anthology reflects on the problematic relationship between the original and its copy which is also relevant to various drafts of a poem. On the one hand, "Itself a copy of lost events,/the original is nowhere."

On the other hand, one finds "dinosaur smells, that leave no copies."

On the one hand, the mythical world of rituals is evoked where an original loses itself for ever leaving no copy behind :

And we have originals, clay tigers
that aboriginal drawn after each small-
pox ritual,

On the other hand, the modern, realistic world is presented where a copy is in search of its original :

adopted daughters researching parents
through maiden names in changing languages,
telephone books,

and familiar grins in railway stations.

And bracketed between this fantastic, mythical and the realistic worlds, it is found that "these words" are like "copies with displaced originals" (*CP* : 158). Like "Which Reminds Me" in *The Striders*, "Drafts" also juxtaposes the fantastic and the realistic in the context of the originality of a poetic text.

Art's encounter with life as the other, tinged with terror, culminates in "The Black Hen" (*CP* : 195), the title poem of Ramanujan's last anthology, *The Black Hen* (1995). The poem begins by echoing Keats's statement about creative process : "It must come as leaves/to a tree/or not at all." And the rest of the poem contradicts this Keatsian, romantic view of creative process by emphasizing conscious, deliberate craftsmanship : "On the embroidery/stitch by stitch/dropped and found again." And when the completed poem is there

the black hen stares
with its round red eye

and you're afraid

Though the use of "you" in the last line of the poem may be generic, it is not farfetched to think in view of the stark objectivity of the completed artifact as a black hen that the poet's self, "I," turns into the other, the second person pronoun, "you." Further, in "The striders," the first poem in the first anthology, it is the poet who perceives the world in the creative process, while in "The Black Hen," the first poem in the last anthology, it is the completed poem, the black hen, which stares at the poet. It is the sense of the otherness and terror in the creative process that makes the red round eyes of a black hen stare at the poet, who is "afraid."

II

Art's encounter with life as the other is expressed through the first form of self-reflexivity in the poems about the creative process. It becomes more pronounced in many of Ramanujan's poems through the second form of self-reflexivity as the negotiation of art and life in various directions.

"A River" (*CP* : 38-39) in *The Striders* responds to the river Vaikai of Madurai, which has been the centre of Tamil culture for the last two thousand years. The poem ironically asserts that only the flooded river is found by the old and the new poets "to be poetic/about only once a year." But in real life this flooded river washes away "one pregnant woman expecting identical twins." And it is callously ignored in the realm of art. "A River" is an ironic statement about dehumanization of art, an art which flourishes at the cost of life. Though the poem reacts to the old as well as the new poets, what Jose' Ortega Y Gasset notes about the modernist movement is pertinent here :

> And when we seek to ascertain the most general and most characteristic feature of modern artistic production we come upon the tendency to dehumanize art (Gasset : 34).

In the duality of art and life, "A River" criticizes art and favours life.

Similarly, "Time to Stop" in *Relations* (1971) warns against too many visits to a museum and too much preoccupation with modern paintings which blunts the sensitive approach to life :

and after an accident,
blood
looks remarkably
like fresh paint.

Then
it's time to stop
going to museums. (*CP* : 82)

Thus, art should not treat superciliously the value of human suffering in life.

Contrary to "A River" and "Time to Stop," "Any Cow's Horn Can Do It" (*CP* : 93-94) in *Relations* (1971) favours art against life. The real circumstances like "any cousin's death" or "Any old quarrel over novel,/movie, or a suspicion/of pregnancy is enough" to make a woman ruminate over it. Even "Any cow's horn tilted at/a child in the street will do it." But any human suffering, framed within an aesthetic object like a poem, would not affect such women :

...Poems aren't even words
enough to rankle, infect
or make the smallest incisions.

Measured against the felt intensity of events in life, the significance of events in arts gets undeservedly minimized. Though W.H. Auden in his elegy on the death of W.B. Yeats states that "poetry makes nothing happen," he does imply that poetry makes much happen at intellectual, moral level.

"He too Was a Light Sleeper Once" (*CP* : 162) in *Second Sight* presents a poet who is not unlike T.S. Eliot's modern man in *The Waste Land* who feels that "April is the cruellest month." The poet, once a light sleeper, had a refined sensibility to respond to the subtle stimuli of life. But now he has undergone acute suffering in life : a "sudden jail," a "long exile," and

marriage of his heart's
little bird
to a clawing cat,
cigarette burns
on children's most private parts.

Instead of encountering life through art as earlier, now he escapes into sound sleep, "to climb again to other slopes of sleep," as his sorrowful life has become too cruel and gross to be available to refined art. With "the iron taste of print in his mouth," the unhappy poet faces the divide between the spheres of art and life.

Thus, a few poems in *The Striders Relations*, and *Second Sight* reflect on the duality of art and life where this duality verges on being a dichotomy of art and life.

"Traces" in *The Black Hen* approaches the pristine, unapproachable reality whose traces today, including the works of art, are human interpretations. The remote stars which are "light years away" belong to a different galaxy and different time, and they are humanized as "the Seven/Sages and the Milky Way" (*CP* : 204). Similarly, the unknowable oceans, the image of life and reality (cf. W.B. Yeats's "Sailing to Byzantium"), are humanized through the works of art like "The Tempest, Moby Dick,/and Robinson Crusoe" (*CP* : 204). Though art's humanization is limited in its embodiment of life, humanization is a condition of art's being.

"Difficulty" (*CP* : 241) discovers the creative potential which lies in the encounter between art and life. Difficulty lies in writing

> anything, when little demons
> throw colours and hunger
> cries tear through the paper
> destroy the commas and devour
> the passive voice.

But it is also true that the clash between creative urge and sorrowful life fructifies "into unlikely leaf/in winter."

"Poetry and Our City" (*CP* : 242) examines with light irony the relative success of different poetic forms in representing contemporary life. The formal rigour of a poetic form fails to embody amorphous life. The "sonnet forms" fail, and "haikus and tankas," being formally more rigorous, fail more. And "free verse," being more flexible, reflects modern chaotic life more successfully, but it sacrifices aesthetic distance and meets "an accident" (*CP* : 242). This poem evaluates a poetic form with respect to its capacity to tackle life.

"No Fifth Man : after an old Sanskrit parable" (*CP* : 243-45) presents four learned brahmans who ignore the warning given by their uneducated boyhood friend and apply art and give life to a tigress's skeleton. The created tigress eats the four brahmans up, leaving the artless fifth man safe on a tree. But

Poetry too is a tigress,
except there's no fifth
man left on a tree
when she takes your breath
away.

The four brahmans, the creators, are finally dehumanized in the creative act. The staring black hen of the title poem, "The Black Hen," transforms itself into a leaping tigress in "No Fifth Man." This poem plays a variation on "Traces." "Traces" asserts that art is based on humanization in a limited way. "No Fifth Man" focuses on the limited nature of humanization and asserts that dehumanization is a condition of art.

"Bulls" (*CP* : 246) begins with a tense, concrete image :

Bulls and bulldozers
block each other
on the road to Chidambaram. (246)

Life ("Bulls") and the artifact based on life, suggested verbally ("bulldozers"), literally encounter each other. The ironic tension between the traditional Indian faith in religion and the contemporary improverished Indian life culminates at the end of the poem in

making language
like early birds
or even this page. (246)

Like "Difficulty," this poem also views the clash between art and life as making poetic language.

"Museum" (*CP* : 256) presents the nocturnal prances of the horses in the Chinese painting. These horses, transformed by art, are "not horses," as "people who appear in dreams/are not themselves" and they prance out of the painting on a wall "to trample the flowers/in the emperor's gardens/night after night." Art not only encounters life, but also accepts it.

"Fear No Fall" (*CP* : 275-77), the last poem in Ramanujan's *Collected Poems,* refers in its first section to the life of a spendthrift and drunkard, who finally throws himself down desperately from a mountainous cliff. But he is saved by an old man, a divine figure. He is graced by the gift of poetry, to be known later as Arunagiri, a Tamil Saint. In the second section, the poem likens in a dreamy state ("That night") a modern poet's required fall from the heap of books to Arunagiri's fall :

> When a voice both within and without
> said, 'Fall, fall,
> you'll never fear a fall again,
> fall now!'

The sense of terror in the creative act as seen in the earlier poems is now accepted wholeheartedly.

Arunagiri's legendary fortunate fall suggests both dehumanization and humanization in art : his attempt to end his life suggests the former, and the way he is saved and initiated into art implies the latter. Thus, art and life are coterminous. But a modern poet requires a fall into life from "a ramshacle pyramid/of all my books" (277). What is required is art's final surrender to life.

The negotiation of art and life works through various poetic strands in Ramanujan's poetry : both dehumanization and humanization as necessary conditions of art's being, the tension between art and life as a creative source, the merger of art and life, and the acute need of art to surrender to life. Moreover, compared to the earlier anthologies like *The Striders, Relations* and *Second Sight, The Black Hen* has more poems which negotiate art and life. Further, the negotiation of art and life in the earlier anthologies verges on being a dichotomy of art and life, but *The Black Hen* works towards a resolution of the dichotomy of art and life.

A.K. Ramanujan's poetic journey starts with "The Striders." It is a closed poetic text with the modernist strategy of a strider, an American water insect, hovering over the watery surface. His poetic journey culminates in "Fear No Fall." It opens up the poetic text. It requires a fall into life, inspired by Arunagiri, a Tamil saint, and not the skilful hovering over a surface by an American water insect.

WORKS CITED

Desai, S.K. 1997. "The Poetry of A.K. Ramanujan's in K.M. George (ed.) *Masterpieces of Indian Literature*, Vol I. New Delhi : National Book Trust.

Gasset, Jose Ortega Y. 1986. "First Instalment on the Dehumanization of Art" in Robert Con Davis (ed.) *Contemporary Literary Criticism : Modernism through Post-Structuralism*. New York : Longman.

Kermode, Frank, 1957. *Romantic Image*. London : Routledge & Kegan Paul.

Ramanujan, A.K. 1995. *The Collected Poems of A.K. Ramanujan* (ed.) Vinay Dharwadker. New Delhi : Oxford Univ. Press. Referred to as *CP* in the text.

6

A.K. Ramanujan's Treatment of Love

—MOHAN RAMANAN

Ramanujan is a love poet in addition to being many other things. His morphogenetic inheritance includes Tamil and its great traditions of love poetry, not to speak of his intimate acquaintance with Vaisnava Bhakti poems which like Bhakti poetry of other kinds has a strong erotic motif. His translations *Speaking of Siva, The Interior Landscape, Poems of Love and War* and *The Hymns for The Drowning* drew heavily on this tradition of spiritual love. However, what is remarkable is that Ramanujan, while he was in spirit faithful to his originals, nevertheless had a fine ear for English, and repeatedly he is able to produce good English poetry. Here is an example from a classical Tamil context. It appears in *The Interior Landscape* :

What She Said...
My lover capable of terrible lies
at night lay close to me
in a dream
That lied like truth.

I woke up, still deceived,
and caressed the bed
Thinking it my lover.

It's terrible. I grew lean
in loneliness,
like a water lily
gnawed by a beetle. (Ramanujan, 1967 : 32)

This is what might be aptly called a 'modernist' imitation of a classical text, and I use 'imitation' in Dr. Johnson's sense as standing for that species of composition which is a middling cross between original composition and translation. Ramanujan's characteristic reticence and restraint lower the temperature of the Tamil heroic past. He has always been suspicious of the large romantic gesture or heroic posturing and in his 'modernist' version, something of this bias comes through. The high-falutin sentiment of Tamil heroic poetry is absent, its rhetoric missing. Many, I am sure, will not like this apparent distortion, but one should see it as an example of an ancient culture being mediated by a contemporary mind and reaching us in the present with its essentials intact, all frills removed. We should be thankful for such poetic mediation.

Ramanujan's translation activity has stood him in good stead and we see in his original English compositions the same method of irony, understatement, wit and formal control, which his translations have. Here is an example entitled 'Still Life' from *The Striders* :

When she lelf me
after lunch, I read
for a while.
But I suddenly wanted
to look again
and I saw the half-eaten
sandwich,
bread,
lettuce and salami,
all carrying the shape
of her life. (*CP* : 12)

This is love poetry informed by a fine sense of particulars recalling William Carlos Williams of our time or Donne of the Seventeenth Century. In poems like this Ramanujan gives us the morphology of love — what it feels like to love and lose and search. The result is that 'Still Life' is one of the finest miniatures produced by Ramanujan — a poem where the Romantic urge to confess is countered by ruthless self-irony.

Something similar could be said of the restrained passion of 'Looking for a Cousin on a Swing' (*CP* : 19) from *Striders* where the first stirrings of sex are felt by the four or five-year old girl and her six or seven-year old cousin who "set himself against her" on the swing :

with every lunge of the swing
she felt him
in the lunging pits
of her feeling;

In later years she looks for the swing in suburbs (and tries to be innocent about it — a contrast to the innocence of early childhood—)

not only on the crotch of a tree
that looked as if it would burst
under every leaf
into a brood of scarlet figs

if someone suddenly sneezed.

The tree symbolism is quite central to Ramanujan as we shall see presently but the point here is the restrained yet passionate treatment of love. The passion is only matched by the pathos and restrained feeling in 'Love Poem for a Wife-I' where the poet speaks of the separation of husband and wife as having to do with unshared childhood. The poem goes back to family history (the idea of the family tree is forever present) and delineates various aspects of childhood the couple know about but have not shared and the poet concludes by saying :

Or we should do as well-meaning
hindus did,

betroth us before birth,
forestalling separate horoscopes
and mothers' first periods,
and wed us in the oral cradle
and carry marriage back into
the namelessness of childhoods. (*CP* : 67)

It would, thus, appear that one clear indication of the power of Ramanujan's work lies in this quality of bilingualism. The reader, familiar with the classical tradition which Ramanujan has internalized will find those echoes in his English verse, and moreover in his treatment of love there is a strong native discourse present. Ramanujan himself has spoken of this as follows :

> English and my disciplines (linguistics, anthropology) give me my 'outer' forms — linguistic, metrical, logical and other such ways of shaping experience; and my first thirty years in India, my frequent visits and field trips, my personal and professional preoccupations with Kannada, Tamil, the classics and folklore give me my substance, my 'inner' forms, images and symbols. They are continuous with each other, and I no longer can tell what comes from where (Parthasarathy : 96).

This is an extraordinarily accurate formulation and with this in mind it should be possible to read his poem entitled 'Love Poem for a Wife and Her Trees' (*CP* : 180-83) from *Second Sight.* The poem is in four parts and it is an intricate argument, cleverly organized and precisely articulated.

Part I begins with the poet addressing the wife and distinguishing her from mother, a fact which the wife at any rate will not let him forget though he cannot always remember. Mother is

> certified dead but living on, close
> to her children, tinkling in glass-bead curtains,
> peacock patterns shivering in three cities.

The description of the glass-beads shivering is, of course, absolutely spot on, and anyone from the South at any rate will have no difficulty in relating to it. The difference between wife and mother is particularly noted

> on panic's zenith, on the unattended
> Ferris wheel rickety in the wind,
> lest I collapse
>
> into a son...

Collapsing into sonhood would mean destroying age-old Dravidian relationships, destroying

> the intricate
> diagrams of Dravidian kinship

where triangles
marry only circles descended
from other triangles and circles
in the notebooks

of anthropologists sitting
on family trees, those topsy-
turvy trees
with their roots in heaven
and branches in the earth.

The reference to anthropologists, family trees and Dravidian kinship provides the 'inner form' to the triplet stanzas of the poem which are the English 'outer forms.'

Part II is focused on the wife and her role as daughter of somebody, to the protagonist's role-play as son of a mother. It is a tautly constructed section. The woman, the protagonist says, reminds him that she is not his daughter, "urban maybe/ but always/present." It saves her from the fate of being possessed by "that Grisly Beard,/that phantom son-in-law," and from her own "heart's madness" and from other repressive things. The possessive nature of the relationship between husband and wife is evoked in this section where the protagonist talks of the husband locking her

deep in my male
and royal coffers,

impregnable wombs of metal, and throw[ing] away the
key in the alligator moat.

Together they would go "out of touch" of the world. The poem evokes the image of the woman pressing her face against a fortieth storey window

in the safe custody of an antiseptic
bubble, [her] spinal cord
will wither —

that stem of all senses, that second tree
with the root at the top, branches branching in limb
and lung,

down to toe, hangnail, and fingertip.

The precision of the imagery, the thorough lack of sentimentality, though not the absence of sentiment, characterize Ramanujan's best work and surely these lines from the poem meet those standards.

Part III continues to explore the sense of sameness and difference in the couple — "you are not me but Another." Ramanujan can carry on an extended metaphorical exploration, a modern equivalent of the old fashioned Homeric or Miltonic simile. The 'another' is

The faraway
stranger who's nearby,

like the Blue Mountain tree in the cuttings
of my garden graft, or its original,
sighted once

up close in my telescope, seasoned and alive
with leaf, bud, monkeys, birds, pendant
bats, parasites

patch of blue scilla lilies in its shade;
exotic who inhabits my space
but migrates

to Panamas of another
childhood; one half of me, often
occupying all,

yet ever ready to call a taxi
and go away...

There is much more in this vein but the point is firmly reinforced that nearness and distance, intimacy and rejection are the binary oppositions which imply one another. Each term in the opposition has its negation. The poem is about the multi-dimensional relationship of husband and wife and so part IV clinches it as follows :

Yet I know you'll play at Jewish mama,
sob-sister, daughter who needs help
with arithmetic,

even the sexpot nextdoor, topless

tree spirit on a temple frieze,
or plain Indian wife

at the village well, so I can play son,
father, brother, macho lover, gaping
tourist, and clumsy husband.

By any standards Ramanujan has written a classic love poem of metaphysical dimensions in which he carries through the twin ideas of a relationship in terms of trees, stems, branches, twigs and so forth. This is love poetry which has a terrible beauty, inclusive, passionate and yet complex. Much of this, I believe, comes from Ramanujan's twin inheritance of English and its outer forms and his native provenance and its inner forms.

WORKS CITED

Parthasarathy, R. (ed.). 1976. *Ten Twentieth-Century Indian Poets*. New Delhi: Oxford University Press.

Ramanujan, A.K. 1995. *The Collected Poems of A.K. Ramanujan* (ed.) Vinay Dharwadker. New Delhi : Oxford University Press. Referred to as *CP* in the text.

———. 1967. *The Interior Landscape*. Bloomington : Indiana University Press, rptd. 1994. New Delhi : Oxford University Press.

7

A Post-Colonial Reading of A.K. Ramanujan's Poetry

—BIJAY KUMAR DAS

A.K. Ramanujan is not easy to read. He combines in him the vision of a folklorist, the insight of a poet and the skill of a translator. Though he is at once an expatriate and a post-colonial poet, he successfully turns the expatriate condition and post-colonial situation to his advantage and brings the image of 'India' alive in his poetry. The purpose of the paper is to evaluate Ramanujan as a post-colonial Indian English Poet, notwithstanding his expatriate condition and status.

A.K. Ramanujan's real life situation makes him both an expatriate and a post-colonial poet. He was born into a well to do family in Mysore in 1929. His father was a mathematician and a noted scholar. Three languages English, Tamil and Kannada were spoken at home. He had his early education at D. Bhanumaiah's High School and then he graduated from Maharaja's College, Mysore with honours in English Literature and thereafter he did his Master's degree at the same institution. He taught English Literature at Quilon, Belgaum and Baroda for eight years. He was a fellow of Deccan College, Poona in 1958-59, and a Fulbright scholar at Indiana University in 1960-62. He obtained his Ph.D. degree in Linguistics from Indian University in 1963. He met a Keralite Syrian Christian woman (a Novelist) whose family had settled in Aden for several years. He fell in love with her and then they got married. Ironically enough the love marriage did not last long. It ended in a divorce. Ramanujan like T.S. Eliot toyed with the idea of becoming a

Buddhist. With this aim in view, he went to Sri Lanka in 1963. The influence of Buddhism on him remained all through his life. He joined as an Assistant Professor of Linguistics, Tamil and Dravidian Languages at the University of Chicago and later on became a Professor in the same department. He lived in Chicago for over three decades till he breathed his last in 1993.

Before the terms 'post-colonial' and 'post-colonialism' became a fashion in 1980s, Ramanujan was known as an Indian English poet and more appropriately an expatriate Indian English poet. But as a trilingual writer, translator and folklorist, Ramanujan has assimilated the cultures of his native land (India) and that of the land of his migration (U.S.A.) and successfully brought alive the indigenous transition and culture in his works. Like Derek Walcott, Ramanujan has made a multicultural commitment and transcended the limitation of an expatriate poet. I am inclined to agree with S.S. Dulai when he underlines this aspect of Ramanujan's poetry in the following words :

> His poetry is born out of the dialectical interplay between his Indian and American experience on the one hand, and that between his sense of his own self and all experience on the other. Its substance is both Indian and Western. Starting from the centre of his sense of self and his Indian experience, his poetry executes circles comprehending ever-wider realities, yet maintaining a perfectly taut connection between its constant, and continuously evolving central vision and the expanding scene before it... (Dulai : 151).

Let me first define post-colonialism in order to establish Ramanujan as a post-colonial poet. Post-colonialism semantically means something that has a concern only with the national culture after the departure of imperial power. But in actual practice, it has to be understood only in reference to colonialism. Like colonialism, post-colonialism is a state of consciousness, a crucial stage in the continuum of our cultural process and self-awareness. Colonialism involves two types of imperialism — political and cultural. Therefore, myth and history, language and landscape, self and the other are all very important ingredients of post-colonialism.

Post-colonial theory states that the major theme of literature from post-colonial countries can be taken as resistance to the former coloniser. It further assumes that the writers who write back to the centre are representing the people of their society authentically. Ramanujan's poetry gives an authentic representation of indigenous tradition, and native culture in artistic terms. His five volumes of poetry — *The Striders* (1966), *Relations* (1971), *Selected Poems* (1976), *Second Sight* (1986) and *The Collected Poems of A.K. Ramanujan* (incorporating *The Black Hen*) (1995) — bear testimony to it.

Ramanujan's vision of life is coloured by his 'Hindu Consciousness.' The ancient tradition of South India shapes his mind and to a large extent determines his attitude to life. His attempt to assimilate the South Indian tradition (particularly Tamil and Kannada tradition) to English becomes successful as he brings 'family,' 'history' and 'mother' into the texture of his poetry. Most of the poems in his first three volumes have their origin in recollected personal emotion and they deal with the poet's memory of his relations and the ambiguous freedom that life away from them confers. In his well known poem, "Small-Scale Reflections on a Great House" (*CP* : 96-99) everything 'lost long ago' revives in the speaker's memory afresh with a touch of nostalgia and pathos. Here we get a catalogue of things that come into the house from outside to stay for ever and the things that go out return inevitably : 'Wandering Cows,' 'library books,' 'neighbour's dishes,' 'the Servants,' 'the Phonographs,' 'the epilepsies in the blood,' 'sons-in-law,' 'daughter-in-law,' 'letters,' 'ideas,' beggar song, widowed daughters, grand children, nephew killed in the war. This is undoubtedly the perfect picture of a joint Hindu family. There is also an undertone of irony in the poem. The title itself is ironical. Children are not blessed into the family and instead, there is vulgarity in the following lines :

lame wandering cows from nowhere
have been known to be tethered.
given a name, encouraged.

to get pregnant in the broad daylight
of the street under the elders'

supervision, the girls hiding
behind windows with holes in them.

Poems such as 'of Mothers, among other things,' 'On the Very Possible Jaundice of an Unborn Daughter,' 'Still Another for Mother,' 'Love Poem for Wife I.' 'History,' 'Looking for a Cousin on a Swing,' 'Obituary' and a few others deal with the family theme. In 'Self Portrait,' his own image resembles —

the portrait of a stranger,
date known,
often signed in a corner
by my father. (*CP* : 23)

This obsession with the family theme finds its expression in his three important poems of *Second Sight.* In 'Extended Family,' the poet recalls his grand-father on the one hand and imagines his great-great-grandson and takes a vow not to be 'dependent/on several people/yet to come.' In 'Love Poem for a Wife and Her Trees' Ramanujan imaginatively perceives three generations of women — mother, wife and daughter in linear progression. His family has its 'roots in heaven/and branches in the earth.' In another Poem called, 'Looking for the Centre' (CP : 184-85) Ramanujan tries to discover his roots and finding it not easy, he tries to extricate himself from this bondage. Thus he says,

Suddenly, connections severed
as in a lobotomy, unburdened
of history, I lose

my bearings, a circus Zilla Spun
at the end of her rope, dizzy
terrified,

and happy . . .

Behind the search for family connections there lies the ground-swell for diving deep in order to discover the roots. The country of his birth haunts his mind without end. Thus, the poet says,

As I transact with the past as with another
country with its own customs, currency,

stock exchange, always
at a loss when I count my change :...
('Waterfalls in a Bank,' *CP* : 189)

Ramanujan being a folklorist, makes use of folklore in his poetry. "No Fifth Man," a poem included in *The Black Hen* tells us about the story of five brahmans who went abroad to study all the sixty four arts, wanted to show off their knowledge by bringing a dead tiger back to life and in the process all but one lost their lives. The fifth one who had commonsense was saved. Ramanujan puts the whole story in its proper perspective.

The fifthman, the coward
cried, "wait, wait
just one second
and climbed up a tree in a hurry

while the fourth chanted a mantra
gave the tigress life...

and the creature pounced on him
his three friends rooted
in their fear, killed them all
and ate them up for starters
Nothing was left of them
not even a bone. (*CP* : 244-45)

In "Mythologies 1," Ramanujan describes the Putana myth (the demon who offered her poisoned breast to Lord Krishna to suck from, in which the demon got a new life in her death). The paradox is that by getting killed in the act of offering poisoned milk to the Lord, she got deliverance from the life of a demon. Thus he writes :

The Child took her breast
in his mouth and sucked it right out of her chest
Her carcass stretched from North to South
She changed, undone by grace
from deadly mother to happy demon
found life in death. (*CP* : 221)

In "Mythologies 2" Ramanujan shows how Lord Vishnu kills a person, howsoever, clever who has got a boon not to be killed :

When the clever man asks the perfect boon :
not to be slain by demon, god, or by
beast, not by day nor by night,
by no manufactured weapon, not out
Of doors nor inside, not in the sky
nor on earth,

Come now come soon,
Vishnu, man, lion, neither and both, to hold
him in your lap to disembowel his pride
with the steel glint of bare claws at twilight.

(*CP* : 226)

Ramanujan's knowledge of Indian myths and folklore is amazing. And he makes use of myths and folklore as themes in his poetry. And it is in this aspect that his poetry conforms to the norm of post-colonial literature.

Ramanujan's poetry closely monitors the relation between nature and the human body and examines the impact of culture and time on this relationship. The interactions of body with the natural world are skilfully worked out in poems like "Love Poem for a Wife and Her Trees" and "Looking for the Centre." Ramanujan maintains that physical reproduction occurs in the branches of 'family trees,' 'with their roots in heaven/and branches in the earth.' He metaphorically says that an 'anatomy of text-book' which unfolds 'a human body, layer/underlayer, skin, muscle, ganglia/of nerves, branching red' is finally put 'into a map of the heavens,' meaning man is inextricably bound to the cosmos. In the significant poem called "One More on a Deathless Theme" included in *The Black Hen* Ramanujan further works out on the theme of 'the body-nature nexus.' The body after death returns to nature. As the poet says :

Everyone in this street
will become cold, lie under stones
or be scattered as ash
in rivers and oceans. (*CP* : 210)

Apart from bringing a correlation between 'body' and 'nature' in his poetry, Ramanujan also points out that 'time' and 'culture' form an integral part of human life. As he puts it :

Time moves in and out of me
a stream of sound, a breeze,
an electric current that seeks
the ground, ...

Morning brown
into evenings before I turn around
in the day. ('Sonnet' *CP* : 220)

Ramanujan like Eliot does not believe that time is linear. It is the cyclic process of life that rotates for ever.

Besides, thematic contents which reveal the identity of Ramanujan as a post-colonial poet, the form and language of his poetry clearly establish this fact. If post-colonial poetry is to be written in English or 'english' as emphasized by the authors of *The Empire Writes Back*, Ramanujan has little to fear. Ashcroft *et al.* assert that 'we distinguish into this account between the 'Standard' British English inherited from the empire and the English which the language has become in the post-colonial countries' (1989 : 8). Ramanujan uses English language with ease and feels comfortable with it. His command of language won encomium from critics. H.C. Harrex's observation on this aspect seems to be valid :

> A.K. Ramanujan used language with a surgeon-like precision, realising that the secret of life is more likely to be found in the smallest rather than the most comic particles of existence....We should note under language that Ramanujan has evolved a personal pliant English which retains its normal power of rational analysis yet is also internalised to achieve a resonance of Indian feeling and Hindu impulse (Harrex : 155).

Reversing Keats's dictum Ramanujan tells us that a poem comes not always as leaves to a tree, but differently one has to work on it. Taking black hen as a metaphor for a poem, he says :

It must come as leaves
to a tree
or not at all

Yet it comes sometimes

as the black hen
with the red round eye

on the embroidery
stich by stich
dropped and found again

and when it's all there
the black hen stares
with its round eye

and you're afraid. (*The Black Hen*, *CP* : 195)

As stated in "Poetry and Our City," Ramanujan while writing poetry 'settles down to free verse.' Not only that, 'irony' becomes a favourite mode in his poetry, like Ezekiel's 'Guru' who is scrupulous in checking the accounts of the Ashram Ramanujan's 'Guru' exploits the disciple and is hypocritical by nature. The 'Guru' in the poem, "The Guru" asked his disciple not to do certain things. Disregarding his advice the protagonist did otherwise :

I gave the dog his bone, the parrot
his seed, the pet snake his mouse

forgave the weasel his tooth
forgave the tiger his claw

and left the guru to clean his shoe
for I remembered I was born of a woman.
(*CP* : 251)

A close reading of Ramanujan's poetry convinces one that it conforms to the norm of 'post-coloniality' both in content and form (*i.e.*, in themes and the use of language). His 'multicultural commitment' (which I mentioned in the beginning of this paper) makes him a true post-colonial poet. He makes it clear in a poem called "Connect" :

Connect ! Connect ! Cries my disconnecting
madness, remembering phrases.
See the cycles.

father whispers in my ear, black holes

and white noise, elections with four-year
shadows, red eclipses

and the statistics of rape. Connect,
connect, beasts with monks, slave economies
and the golden bough. (*CP* : 178)

To conclude, I should say that by re-creating characters in their own situation, and by bringing an indigenous culture alive in English language, Ramanujan adapts himself to the post-colonial situation and thus becomes a significant post-colonial poet, who himself is 'the unity of his work.'

WORKS CITED

Ashcroft, Bill, *et al.* 1989. *The Empire Writes Back*. London : Routledge.

Dulai, Surjit S. 1989. "First and Only Sight : The Centre and Circles of A.K. Ramanujan's Poetry." *Journal of South Asian Literature*, 24, 1-2 (Summer/Fall) : 149-75.

Harrex, C. 1980. "Small Scale Reflections on Indian English Language Poetry." *Journal of Indian Writing in English*, 8, 1-2 (Jan.-Dec.) : 136-56.

Ramanujan, A.K. 1995. *The Collected Poems of A.K. Ramanujan* (ed.) Vinay Dharwadker. New Delhi : Oxford University Press. Referred to as *CP* in the text.

8

Locating A.K. Ramanujan : Memory, Self and Identity in His Poetry

—E.V. RAMAKRISHNAN

Besides being a poet, A.K. Ramanujan has also been a translator, a linguist, an editor and a folklorist. He has written on a wide variety of topics relating to poetry and culture. All these disciplines have left their mark on his poetry. He has observed : "English and my disciplines give me my outer forms — linguistic, metrical, logical and other such ways of the shaping of experience" (Cited in Parthasarathy : 96). He traces his "inner forms" to his Indian childhood and his preoccupations with Kannada, Tamil, the classics and folklore. What he does not mention is that the inner and outer worlds have a tense relationship born of their different orientations. His poetry can be seen as an attempt to interrogate the set patterns of these (outer) discursive disciplines and integrate them within a more inclusive (inner) world-view. Poetry obviously must have been greatly liberating for him as it afforded a means of getting out of closed worlds and forced conclusions. His poems reveal the presence of a tireless investigator who distances himself from stereotyped notions of the self and modernity. He does not see himself as an expatriate writer who has no use for his native traditions. Nor is he a nativist who celebrates the rootedness of cultures. He does not renounce one world for another. It is instructive to view him as a poet-translator who moved between cultures and languages constantly. Translation for him was a creative mode of constructing his word and defining his personal world. In this sense, translation helps us understand his creative strategies. Ramanujan once described himself as the hyphen in the word "Indo-American." Translation as a creative process helps us see the world of the hyphen as a mode of mediation. In writing poetry he could incorporate this hyphenated identity into his intellectual world and give it substance. As a poet who lived on the borderland of several languages and cultures, he saw marginality as an essential condition of this "hyphenated" existence. But the exile can use his memory as a way of resisting marginality and recovering identity. Poetry made it possible for him to return to the resources of memory and see things differently. Poetry was for him as much the art of seeing as the art of saying. As will be seen in the discussion below, several of his poems problematise the very acts of remembering and seeing.

Memory is not central to the first volume *The Striders* which represents the modernist phase of Ramanujan's poetry. In poems like "Breaded Fish," "Still Another for Mother," "Looking for a Cousin on a Swing" memory functions largely like moments of epiphany when something is suddenly revealed. The resources of memory are still repressed and are not available for narration. The poet is still trapped in the world of discrete objects where connections are few and far between. "A Poem on Particulars," the penultimate poem in the first volume, illustrates the nature of the conflict in this type of verse. The wicker-basket that holds oranges arrests the poet's attention in the market-place. The "pellmell piled" oranges open up a rich world of organic colours and shapes. Some green, others with just a finger-print of green, some pulpy and valvet-skinned — the act of seeing becomes progressively complicated as we enter the inside world of the orange. Here we notice the grandpa grip of its fibrous fabric. From this densely patterned inner world we move to the outer tree which pours its future from forgotten roots to feed "this Fall-minded pot-bellied bud till it rounded for our baskets" (*CP* : 53). The "human umbilicus" which binds the fruit with the tree also connects it with the earth. But Ramanujan does not seem to be concerned with their 'fall.' The "vegetal radicalism" (Burke : 81) we find in poets like Theodore Roethke, who discovers a self-sufficient and organic world in plants, totally independent of the human world, is missing here. There is no search for an uncontaminated state in which objects exist in a pristine condition. Ramanujan's modernity has to be located here as a way of incorporating the world of the market and the fall it implies, into his field of vision. In the final stanza, Ramanujan reverts to the paradoxical wisdom of popular saying which neither accepts nor rejects the contradictions between the rooted tree and the plucked fruit : "I have heard it said/among planters:/ you can sometimes count/every orange/on a tree/but never/all the trees/in a single orange" (*CP* : 54). The central paradox of the poem is the mutually exclusive worlds that do not enter into each other. They can only be ironically juxtaposed. In the popular saying at the end of the poem, however, there is an attempt to go beyond the empirical. It is in the collective wisdom of the community that the particulars are recovered as part of the whole. Such a possibility is hinted but not realized in this poem. The baskets of oranges in the market, their tightly textured insides, the green world of the orchard where they hang from the branches and finally the planters' remarks — Ramanujan does not grade these worlds and establish a hierarchical relationship between them.

In his book, *Ways of Seeing*, John Berger comments that the convention of perspective which is unique to European art, makes the single eye "the centre of the visible world" (Berger : 16). In the above poem, the perspective used by Ramanujan is largely unitary as the visible world is viewed from a single perspective. When he reverts to speech at the end of the poem the ocular centrality of the poem is offset to some extent but not subverted entirely. The illusion fostered by a single perspective can be offset only when alternative fields of vision enter the poem. It has been observed that one of the major influences on Ramanujan's early poetry was William Carlos Williams. A poem like "The Striders" carries the stamp of Williamsian ideology which was concerned with the minute details of the objective world. But as Ramanujan developed as a poet he could see the limitations of such an imagistic ordering of reality. He felt the need to comment and interpret. His search for an alternative poetic can be seen in his subsequent volumes when he makes efforts to order his poems around a different logic.

In his second volume *Relations,* memory becomes an organizing principle. Memory in these poems does not suggest a point of origin with reference to which everything becomes significant. On the contrary, it recovers a dimension of the present which would otherwise be lost. In a poem like "Small-scale Reflections on a Great House" the self is not seen in terms of discrete objects but as part of a web of relationships. The poem does not use a linear perspective. A line such as "nothing that ever comes into this house goes out" is followed by a list of things which come into the house to lose their identity and become part of a common tradition. This assimilative character of the house makes a difference to everything that is "housed" inside. Anything that goes out "comes back, processed and often with long bills attached." The mystery of the house deepens as the poem progresses till the great house takes on the character of memory itself. It accommodates, transforms and waits. Vinay Dharwadker sees the poem as a "national allegory" that "uncovers suggestive parallels between the family's fortunes and the modern social history of middle class and upper caste India as a whole" (*CP* : XXX). But this reading seems to miss the tension between the great and the small in the title. In his "Introduction" to *The Speaking of Siva,* Ramanujan while speaking of the traffic between great and little traditions comments : "But traditions are not divided by impermeable membranes; they interflow into one another, responsive to differences of density as in an osmosis" (Ramanujan, 1973 : 23). House is a site of interpenetration of the public and the private where history and biography meet. It resists abstractions. "Nation" is an abstraction which erases several levels of complex identity which are significant sources of meaning. The house apprehends memory in spatial terms. The poem does not privilege grand narratives and thus resists the allegorical impulse which is assimilative and reductive. That which is timeless, universal and elitist meets here its opposites namely transient, parochial and common.

The metaphor of the house in Ramanujan functions as memory in several other poems as well. In "Love Poem for a

Wife 1" the poet says : "Really what keeps us apart/at the end of years is unshared childhood." Shared memories point to a common identity. In this sense, culture is memory because it makes possible access to a common language of experience. In his Kannada poem, "When an Old Familiar Thing Comes Home Again," the past is seen as something that cannot be accommodated in the present. The baby elephant he played with passes by his house. He is happy that the elephant doesn't remember him. When he sends the mahout and the elephant away with some gifts, he feels his house has turned small. The optics of memory transforms the dimensions of his existence. Here, the old man's relation with the past changes significantly. In an interview Robert Lowell once observed : "From year to year, things remembered from the past change almost more than the present" (Lowell : 113). A.K. Ramanujan's poems are also about the complication of memory by one's engagement with the present.

In the poem "On Memory," Ramanujan describes the conflict between "Memory" and "memories" : "Memory, in a crowd of memories, seems to have no place at all for unforgettable things." The desire for transcendence and its impossibility in our own times is what animates a paradoxical statement like this. There are moments which cannot be abstracted and stored in the great Memory which in course of time becomes a dumping ground of unusable past. It is "the unforgettable things" that constitute the self and define one's identity. As opposed to the static and mechanical memory which merely stores information, these "memories" constitute an inner continuity, making it possible to connect the present self with the past. 'Memories' make epiphanies possible because their significance is in the present. It is the invisible third dimension of our identity. This is particularly true of exiles for whom memory is a country they carry with them. In "A Lapse of Memory" the poet speaks of the loss of memory as the loss of identity. The amnesiac is a stranded man in a world of objects which he cannot relate to. What he misses is the sense of significance that only the past can retrieve. In "No Amnesiac King," he feels lost in the city but does not want to seek the magic ring that will restore him to a world of lost connections. Ramanujan seems to think that modernity fosters selective memory by creating vast areas of amnesia. The Amnesiac King demystifies the transcendental power of memory. When seeing is not informed by memory the act of seeing becomes mere witnessing. This state of being is described in "The Watchers" (*CP* : 137). The watchers impose nothing and take no positions. They are people who remain "unwitting witnesses" and "mere seers" because they merely watch without remembering. Memory can become empowering when it transforms what is seen. In "Elements of Composition" what is remembered becomes the self : "I pass through them as they pass through me," and "and even as I add,/I lose, decompose/ into my elements,/into other names and forms/past, and passing, tenses/without time,/caterpillar on a leaf, eating/being eaten" (*CP* : 123). One is composed by what one goes through. The word-play on 'composition' is deliberate as it also refers to the act of writing poetry. The act of looking can be a hallucinatory experience when it is not informed by memory. Modern urban culture encourages spectacles of floating images. From advertisements and comics to museums and zoos, modern institutions regulate our visual experience. In the poem "In the Zoo" which has the subtitle 'a tour with comments' every animal occasions comments which relate them to the poet's past experiences. The faded black colour of adjutant stork reminds the poet of the Madras lawyers and the flight of these birds recall several instances of the past related to his father. What would have been a series of still lives is thus transformed into a dialogic frame of interpenetrating thoughts.

The hallucinatory nature of images which are not informed by memory is brought out by the "Highway Stripper." This poem is about the voyeuristic nature of modern urban culture that encourages amnesia through alluring images. In "Highway Stripper" (*CP* : 163-66) the speaker in the poem, while speeding in his car on the highway to Mexico, sees (or so he thinks) a woman in a speeding car ahead of him strip herself of all clothes. She throws away her hat, skirt, blouse, bra and panties one after the other. Egged on by excitement and curiosity, he overtakes the car and peers into the vehicle as they are level : "In that absolute/second,/that glimpse and after-/image in this hell/of voyeurs, I saw/only one at the wheel:/a man, about forty,/a spectacled profile/looking only/at the road/beyond the nose/of his Mustang,/with a football radio on." There was no trace of a woman in the car. The middle-aged man in the car is one of the countless strangers you see on the road everyday. The speaker is at a loss to decide whether it was the man at the wheel shedding the woman he was wearing. Then the poem reaches its climax as it turns inward and exclaims : "or was it me/moulting, shedding/vestiges,/old investments,/rushing forever/ towards a perfect/coupling/with naked nothing/in a world/without places?" The whole scene has elements of the surreal. That the incident takes place on a speeding automobile moving from one country to another is significant. Speed is characteristic of western culture which values mobility as a means of transcendence. But the speaker in the poem is a prisoner of images as he has no means of liberating himself from the clutches of desire. Voyeurism is debilitating as it seeks to possess, own and devour. In "Highway Stripper" female sexuality is seen as an object of voyeuristic desire. It finally terminates into a moment of anxiety and despair. "A perfect coupling with naked nothing in a world without places" suggests a sense of homelessness as release from the oppressiveness of time and place does not materialize.

While commenting on the Indian and Oriental traditions in painting, Gulammohammad Sheikh remarks : "Being essentially an outdoor vision, most Indian and Oriental painting in general is independent of the windowed view; and this among other reasons renders illusionism unsuitable for pictorial expression" (Sheikh : 146). The murals are characteristically Indian in that they require the spectator to move about while scanning the vast expanse crowded with shapes, figures and images of various kind. Ramanujan's poetry moves towards this kind of a logic as his poems become panels of images directing our gaze towards various planes without emphasizing one at the cost of another. In the poem "The Second Sight" he asserts that the only sight he owns is the first one, the physical sight. The sensory experience is indeed the base of all imaginative experiences.

In "Looking for Centre" he remarks that only eccentrics will look for the centre. In the anatomy book one comes across a map of heavens among the interiors of the body. The self is not perceived here as a perpetually missing centre as Vinay Dharwadker comments but a thing of flux which is constantly modified by the outer world. The act of looking becomes problematic in a world where meanings are prefabricated. "Traces" is another poem that reveals the paradoxical nature of vision itself. Ramanujan seems to suggest that much of what we see is the result of our location : "The stars are constellations only to an eye light years away." The astronomer knows that what he sees is already past because the light which falls on his eye began its journey light years ago and during that time entire galaxies must have disappeared. Everything from fossils to cowskull leaves traces which when deciphered "give themselves a past and a family tree" (*CP* : 204). Ramanujan's "outer" disciplines had something to do with the act of deciphering the 'traces' of the past. From anthropology to folklore, the disciplines he pursued dealt with collective memory at various levels.

The oral poetics of the medieval Kannada "vachanas" is something that relies on the unmediated vision based on personal vision and experience. In his introduction to *Speaking of Siva,* Ramanujan says : "Like European Protestants, the Virasaivas returned to what they felt was the original inspiration of the ancient traditions no different from true and present experience" (Ramanujan 1973 : 33). What the medieval bhakti poets do is to problematise our habits of seeing. Defiance is their way of resisting commonsense. They use everyday experiences as metaphors and reveal something which was never clearly seen or understood. For instance, a famous *vachana* by Basavanna beings by saying that "the sacrificial lamb brought for the festival/ ate up the green leaf brought for the decorations." The statement is concrete and factual and something based on the poet's experience. The second stanza is about the lamb's ignorance of its own fate. The operative word here is "not knowing" because the poem is about the process of knowing. The third stanza questions our own fate : "But tell me : did the killers survive, O lord of the meeting rivers?" This question forces us to see ourselves as the sacrificial lambs. An awareness of our own essential vulnerability becomes empowering since it makes us see the world in a different light. When the self steps out from its habitual frames of seeing, it sees itself as part of a larger world. In her discussion of Kabir's *ultabhamsi* ("upside-down language") Linda Hess says : "What is being transformed is the very apparatus of thinking. Somehow the instrument is made to measure itself, the eye to see itself, the sword to cut itself" (Hess, *et al.* : 145). This is a struggle to redefine oneself, to see oneself from outside and to come to terms with the contraries of existence. In "Contraries" (*CP* : 230) the images of paradoxes finally lead the poet to exclaim : "Beauty is now ugly, sad is glad,/truth are lies/when, living by contraries, his roots are topsyturvy trees."

This vision of contraries also occasions poems like "Foundlings in the Yukon" which is about the accidental discovery of some seeds by some miners in one of the coldest regions of the earth. Within forty eight hours of their being planted, these seeds which lay frozen in the bowels of the earth for thousands of years "drank up the sun," and "unfurled early." Later they flowered much faster than "a modern Alaskan lupine." They were perhaps answering "the kick and shift of an intra-uterine memory." This memory is "radical" in the sense it is more like a genetic code inscribed on the chromosomes of the cell's nuclei. Here memory becomes biological, transformative and regenerative. We may recall the house in the "Small-scale Reflections on a Great House" which also nurtures and waits. These plants become the youngest and the oldest at the same time : "these infants compact with age,/older than the oldest/things alive, having skipped/a million falls/and the registry of tree-rings,/suddenly younger/by an accident of flowering/than all their timely descendants." As in "Traces" we are struck by the paradoxical experience of time.

Poems like "Traces," "Contraries" and "Foundlings in the Yukon" view the self as a process rather than a product. The self is in the making even as it is interacting with the world. In these poems frames flow into each other and the self is seen as a fluid field, and not as a fixed centre. Art and life interpenetrate and destroy their autonomies. In "The Black Hen" this interpenetration takes place at another level as the created image takes on a life of its own. The poem is about "it" ("It must come as leaves/to a tree"), the other which can be only obliquely apprehended. When "it" is finally given expression through art it threatens the stability of the self. However, this poem is not typical of the later Ramanujan who is deeply concerned with ethical questions in life. "The Black Hen" sees art as skill and craft and not as divine inspiration. The transformation of Arunagiri, the Tamil saint, comes through a fall. At the end of a ruined life, he jumped from a precipice to land on the lap of a saint who gave him his first line of verse before disappearing: "leaving Arunagiri a lifetime/of seeking and finding and losing Him/again and again in a labyrinth/of winding words, his songs/ twining around trees, ensnaring/passersby, unlocking cages/even for mynahs and parrots." In a dream the poet had that night, he finds himself "tottering without a foothold/on a ramshackle pyramid/of all my books piled any which way/on to a horse cart." A voice from within and without asks him to fall so that he will never fear a fall again. The revelation comes from the fall into "a labyrinth of winding words." There is a certain humility which is characteristic of much of bhakti poetry in accepting the inevitability of fall. One needs to break out of one's prefabricated images to accept the world as it is.

WORKS CITED

Berger, John. 1972, *Ways of Seeing*. Penguin.

Burke, Kenneth. 1950. "The Vegetal Radicalism of Theodore Roethke," *Sewance Review*, 58, 1 : 81.

Hess, Linda and Sukdev Singh. 1986. *The Bijak of Kabir*. Delhi : Motilal Banarasidas.

Lowell, Robert. 1977. "After Reading Five or Six Essays on Me," *Salmangudi*, 37 (Spring) : 113.

Parthasarathy, R. (ed.). 1976. *Ten Twentieth-Century Indian Poets*. New Delhi : Oxford University Press.

Ramanujan, A.K. 1995. *The Collected Poems of A.K. Ramanujan* (ed.) Vinay Dharwadker. New Delhi : Oxford University Press, Referred to as *CP* in the text.

———, 1973. Harmondsworth : *Speaking of Siva*. Penguin.

Sheikh, Gulammohammed. 1993. "The Viewer's View : Looking at Pictures in Tejaswini Niranjana *et al.* (eds.). *Interrogating Modernity : Culture and Colonialism in India*. Seagull.

9

'Family' as a Central Metaphor in A.K. Ramanujan's Poetry

—JAYAPRAKASH A. SHINDE

Metaphor is traditionally taken to be the most fundamental form of figurative language. Terence Hawkes defines figurative language as 'language which doesn't mean what it says' and adds further, "Figurative language deliberately interferes with the system of literal usage. The *interference* takes the form of *transference*, or 'carrying over,' with the aim of achieving a new wider, 'special' or more precise meaning" (Hawkes : 2). Sometimes, the transference takes the form of a part of something being 'carried over' to stand in place of the whole thing. In this sense, in the context of A.K. Ramanujan's poetry, 'family' is the central metaphor, standing for 'society' at large. This highly personal connection is just barely visible to the reader. It may be said that the metaphor of 'family' realizes Ramanujan's personal responses to the world. The chief use of metaphor is to *extend* language in order to expand reality. Ramanujan extends the metaphor to *expand* the reality of family into the reality of society.

The family is the most important unit of social organization. There is no known society in which the family does not comprise an integral part of the social structure. Family patterns of behaviour are related to the norms of the society of which the family forms part; and, moreover, they tend to uphold the normative patterns of that society. There is a mutual interacting and supportive relationship in this respect between the family and society. There are great variations in the internal organization of individual family units. There are differences in family organization even in the same society between different social strata. Nevertheless, the family performs different functions in the maintenance of the social structure. It provides population replacement and it acts as an agent of socialization. The family may be regarded as an institution interrelated with other social institutions or a relatively autonomous social system, itself made up of interacting elements. For many of us, the family constitutes our first experience of social life and for many also, it is the most enduring and permanent social group. In his poetry, Ramanujan is concerned with family life within the context of a wider social structure. My primary interest in this essay is to study Ramanujan's poetry in order to explain how human behavior as it relates to the family enables us to achieve a fuller understanding of the processes at work in society.

The family, which is fully functional as a social institution, tends to be extended vertically to include three or more generations and horizontally to include collateral relations. But, due to the impact of industrialization and urbanization, nowadays, 'extended' multi-generation families living under one roof are less common and the 'nuclear' family of husband, wife, and their children is more common, than in the past. In Ramanujan's poetry, we come across his reflections on his own 'nuclear' family and also the 'extended' family he remembers as he 'transacts with the past' ('Waterfalls in a Bank,' *CP* : 189-90). However, as we browse among his nostalgic reflections, his preference for the 'extended' family becomes quite evident.

Ramanujan's nuclear family consists of him, his wife, and their children. The institution of marriage is central to the idea of the family in most societies; it formalizes and regularizes the relationships between family members. For both sexes emotional security and warmth are important. They can be found in a good marriage relationship. Ramanujan, however, talks of uncertainties in relation to marriage. Social structure remains hierarchical and this is reflected in family life which is patriarchal. Marriage is not considered as a partnership of equals; rather it is viewed as a contract with a strict definition of masculine and feminine roles, together with an equally strict allocation of male and female tasks; and a good marriage is supposed to be one in which both spouses carry out their obligations. Typically, the wife's activities are defined strictly in terms of the husband's convenience and pleasure. Relationship between marriage partners, as revealed in Ramanujan's poems, is not a 'joint' relationship which means 'togetherness' in all aspects of living, but a 'segregated' relationship, which seems to be the inevitable consequence of male indifference. In 'Routine Day Sonnet' (*CP* : 68), the wife cries her heart out 'as if from a crater/in hell;' and the husband realizes : "she hates me, I hate her." In 'Love Poem for a Wife-1' (*CP* : 65-67), the poet refers to the estrangement between him and his wife because of their 'unshared childhood.' They cannot share each other's past. While seeing the family album, she is surprised to see his father 'in a turban,/mother standing on her bare/splayed feet, silver rings/ on her second toes,' and concludes, to his displeasure, that his present self is a sentence from his father's diary. He envies her past, her village dog-ride and the mythological stories of 'the seven crazy aunts.' He does not like to be reminded of the night when her father paced to and fro in the balcony anxiously smoking cigarettes and waiting for his daughter who had gone out on a date with a Muslim friend 'who only hinted at touches.' He is angry when she quarrels with her brother James over the location of the bathroom in her grandfather's house in Alleppey :

> ...Sister-in-law
> and I were blank cut-outs
> fitted to our respective
> slots in a room
> really nowhere...

The thought of being totally obliterated from her world hurts the male ego in him and, embittered, he reflects :

> ...Probably
> Only the Egyptians had it right :
> their kings had sisters for queens...
> Or we should do as well-meaning
> hindus did,

betroth us before birth...
and carry marriage back into
the namelessness of childhood.

As this would never come into practice, Ramanujan seems to suggest, it is impossible to experience 'togetherness' in marriage. At times, as revealed in 'Love Poem for a Wife-2,' he thinks that through his wife he can be 'androgynous as a god,' but he is also aware that the happiness this thought brings to him is but transitory and that with 'past still there, /a dying/ net on the mountain,' he will again be his separate self. In 'Love Poem for a Wife and Her Trees' (*CP* : 180-83). Ramanujan once again asserts the 'segregation' in marriage :

I forget at night and remember at dawn
you're not me but Another, the faraway
stranger who's nearby...

The disharmony and the ensuring disillusionment is, the poet thinks, due to :

...Dravidian kinship
where triangles
marry only circles descended
from other triangles...

In fact, the ideal marital relationship would be the one in which, alongwith 'togetherness,' each one has right to 'singleness,' as illustrated in D.H. Lawrence's novels *The Rainbow* and *Women in Love*. But in Ramanujan's poems, the wife is not allowed to be 'Another.' She is not allowed to have separate identity of her own. The husband expects the wife to be, forever, merely an appendage to him. It is obvious that Ramanujan has used the word 'Love' in the titles of these poems ironically. Love, according to Alex Comfort, includes not only physical attraction and satisfaction, but also 'mutual respect, mutual communication and a strong desire to protect one another without any corresponding wish to manipulate or mould' (Comfort : 88).

Children are, mostly, regarded as a near essential ingredient of a full marriage relationship. It is the family that undertakes the socialization of the child during his long period of dependency. In the family setting, the child first learns to handle some of the different types of personal relationships that he will find later in the wider society. The family, as an agent of social control, teaches the child the limits of tolerated behavior. It introduces him to the acceptable ideas of right and wrong. The parents prepare their children, by means of training and instruction, for life in society. In process of time, they tend to regard parenthood as a means of emotional gratification. Ramanujan, disappointed in his wife, gets emotionally attached to his children. In 'Some Relations' (*Relations*), he fondly remembers his daughter's turtles trying 'to hibernate in the jar, vary far/from the ocean, beginning to be confused/by the heat of this Chicago winter.' One of the 'Entries for a Catalogue of Fears' (*CP* : 86-87) is about his fear regarding his daughter's safety :

> Sudden knives and urchin laughter
> in the red light alley,
> add now
> the men in line
> behind my daughter.

In the changed social condition and atmosphere, the men chasing his daughter add fear in his mind. He loves his children to such a great extent that after death, he will 'do them infinite harm/ staying on the roof/a peeping-tom ghost/looking for all sorts of proof/for the presence of the past' which, we may add, was not as menacing as the present is. The same fear, in 'Son to Father to Son' (*Second Sight*), is the source of his dreams in which he sees his son 'skewered by a bamboo arrow in a jungle trap' and his daughter 'lowered like a match into sulphur mine of hungry men.' Every loving father is haunted by such fear.

Ramanujan chooses a poem translated from a Classical Tamil Anthology, 1st -3rd Centuries A.D., as the epigraph for his second volume *Relations* in *Collected Poems.* The epigraph quotes : "But living/among relations/binds the feet." But the poet cannot escape from his 'relations.' He realizes : "Connections severed..../I lose my bearings" ('Looking for the Centre,' *Second Sight*) and "Connect! Connect! cries my disconnecting/madness" (Connect!). As he says, 'a hood/of memory like a coil on a heath' ('Breaded Fish,' *The Striders*) unfolds itself in his mind and he is back in his 'first thirty years' which have given him his 'substance,' his 'inner' forms (Cited in Parthasarathy : 96). Rama Jha quotes Ramanujan's acknowledgement of 'the roots,' which have provided 'nourishment' to his writing. He admits :

> The past never passes. Either the individual past or historical past or cultural past. It is *with* us. It is that gives us the richness of — what you call it — the richness of understanding. And the richness of expression (Jha : 7).

In his case, the evocation of 'past' is invariably associated with the social documentation of the Hindu 'joint' or 'extended' family in rural setting.

Common values permeate the whole rural complex. Loyalty to family, which is strong, manifests itself in a greater respect for tradition than in urban conditions. Ramanujan's 'extended' family in India comprised parents, grandparents, brothers, sisters, aunts, uncles and cousins. The poet narrates episodes involving these members of his family in so great a detail that he seems to re-live them through memory. As M.K. Naik observes,

> It is not 'emotion recollected in tranquillity' but recollection emotionalized in untranquil moments that appears to be the driving force behind much of Ramanujan's Poetry (Naik : 15).

The 'untranquil moments' refer to the poet's voluntary 'exile' in America, which he can sustain only through 'recollection emotionalized' of the tranquil family-life in India.

It is the house which is the focal point in fostering joint family activity. The Great House in 'Small-Scale Reflections on a Great House' (*Relations*) is eternally receptive. Each and everything that goes in ('lame wandering cows,' 'unread library books,' 'neighbour's dishes,' 'sons-in-law who quite forget their mothers,' 'women who come as wives') remains inside forever. Anything that goes out comes back after sometime, being processed 'like the hooped bales of cotton/shipped off to invisible Manchesters.' And if anyone goes out ('daughters married to short-lived idiots,' 'sons who run away'), he comes back after some period. Everything loses its separate existence in its wholeness. Ramanujan, here, refers to both the tight-knitness of Indian family life and also the security of closeness it offers.

The House encourages community spirit. Participation in such community ceremonies as 'the wedding anniversary of a god' establishes the importance of the family as an agent of social cohesion.

In 'Elements of Composition' (*Second Sight*), Ramanujan refers to 'father's seed and mother's egg' as contributing to his composition. There are quite a few poems in which he writes about his father and his mother. Sometimes, his portrayal of his father approximates to sardonic sarcasm; but he describes his mother always with love, admiration and adoration. 'A Wobbly Top' (*Relations*) explores Ramanujan's emotional relationship with his father. They both had similar temperaments. His father gave him a top to compensate for the quarrel. He compared himself with the top and felt that he also had scars of imperfection, which were temporarily lost in the fast spinning of it. He nostalgically remembers his father 'into the rain, his baggy umbrellas with three ribs/broken by his sons in a fencing match and three/by last year's winds,' his 'Magic Carpet Story' and he 'mopping the kitchen' when the mother was ill ('In the Zoo,' *Second Sight*). He remembers also his father's habit of slapping soap on his back and thinking 'in proverbs' ('Extended Family'). In 'Son to Father to Son,' Ramanujan refers to how, at the age of five, he used to dream of father 'his beard a hanging hive' and scream 'at the hair on his hands/as they held me close/to ask me why.' In 'Obituary' (*Relations*), he ponders, ironically, over the domestic responsibilities left by his dead father : "Father, when he passed on/left dust/on a table full of papers/left debts and daughters,/a bedwetting grandson/named by the toss of a coin after him/a house that leaned/slowly through our growing/years on a bent coconut/tree in the yard." The sarcasm continues in the details about the cremation : "Being the burning type,/he burned properly." The ashes and the bones were thrown 'where three rivers met' in the midst of mantric recitations, as the customs demanded, but no memorial was erected in his honour. Though his father 'did't quite/manage to do himself' anything, "he got two lines/in an inside column/ of a Madras newspaper/sold by the kilo/exactly four weeks later to street-hawkers." The poet didn't feel any loss at the death of his father. It is obvious from the ironical details that he doesn't have much regard for his father. What concerns him more is 'a changed mother' left behind by his father — a widow condemned to an abject plight in a Hindu household.

The mother has always been, through the initial biological closeness between her and the child, the focus of warmth and affection. She symbolizes the integration of the family. In 'Of Mothers, among other things' (*Relations*). Ramanujan discusses his deep attachment for the mother. When he sees his mother — her hands like 'a wet eagle's/two black pink-crinkled feet,' her saris not clinging but hanging like 'loose feather of a onetime wing' and her four still sensible fingers slowly flexing 'to pick a grain of rice from the kitchen floor,' an early memory brings back to him the image of the mother as a young lady — wearing diamond ear rings, running back 'from rain to the crying cradles.' The transformation that time has brought about in the mother so overwhelms him that he says, "My cold parchment tongue licks bark/in the mouth.' In 'Ecology' (*Second Sight*), he is angry at the Red Champak trees that have given Mother the blinding migraine. But Mother would not let them cut down a flowering tree so that it may continue giving 'her gods and her daughters/ and daughter's daughters basketfuls/of annual flower.' Throughout the poem, the poet uses capital letter M for mother. She is the archetypal Mother who selflessly cares for her children. She is very much like the mother in Nissim Ezekiel's well-known poem 'Night of the Scorpion' who says :

> Thank God the scorpion picked on me
> and spared my children. (Ezekiel : 131)

'History' (*Relations*) discusses the other side of this relationship the total lack of affection between parents and children, with reference to the grandaunt and her daughters. Ramanujan's little aunt, unperturbed by 'deaths and children's failures,' 'now carries a different face.' He had been an innocent eyewitness to her heartlessness. On the day when his great aunt died, while he was looking for a green ball, he saw his little dark aunt 'looking for something' under the cot. After many years, he learnt from his mother that on the day the great aunt died, her two daughters "unknown each to the other/alternately picked their mother's body clean.../of diamond ear-rings,/bangles, anklets, the pin/in her hair,/the toe-rings from her wedding/the previous century,/all except the gold/in her teeth..." Their greed for gold did not prevent them from dishonouring even their mother's dead body. It's possible that their mother had not been affectionate to them when they were children. Affection or attachment has to be mutual; if it is not reciprocated, it fades away gradually.

'Snakes' (*The Striders*) are 'like some terrible aunt.' Ramanujan's mother used them in rituals. He was no much afraid of the snakes that even in his sister's braided long hair he imagined them. He could get rid of the fear only when he trampled on a snake and killed it. He remembers 'A Leaky Tap After a Sister's Wedding' (*The Striders*) and also sister 'swinging high/on the creaky swings' ('Son to Father to Son,' *Second Sight*) and 'the look/of panic on sister's face/an hour before/her wedding' ('Elements of Composition'). In 'Saturday,' the poet recalls : 'A brother's briar pipe chatters/between his teeth,/as his heart comes to a stop.' The relationship is extended to other members of the 'joint' family. Flamingoes remind him of 'long-legged aunts in white cottons' and black-faced monkeys of 'grave lowbrow uncles with movable scalps and wrinkled long black hands' ('Zoo Gardens Revisited,' *Second Sight*). Ramanujan describes 'we' as 'our uncle's nephews' ('Real Estate,' *Relations*). He cannot forget an "uncle's eleven fingers/making shadow plays of, rajas/and cats, hissing,/becoming fingers again." ('Elements of Composition,' *Second Sight*) and also another uncle's epilepsies which filled him with 'hymns and twitches' ('Drafts'). While 'Looking for a Cousin on a Swing' (*The Striders*), Ramanujan learns how the innocent physical context of childhood develops into adult sexuality, how the Song of Experience differs considerably from the Song of Innocence. He describes 'the naked Chicago bulb' as 'a cousin of the Vedic Sun,' thus bringing together the East and the West ('Extended Family,' *Second Sight*).

The multi-generation family structure offers the grandparents a function in life. The children are considerably benefited by a close and often indulgent relationship with their grandparents.

The sight of a dirty white stork reminds Ramanujan of 'grandmother's maggoty curds' ('In the Zoo,' *Second Sight*). He sees the bentover grandmother as 'black and wrinkled as raisin' ('Waterfalls in a Bank'). When uncle killed a scorpion, the grandmother told them how a pregnant scorpion would look for a warm secret place and then would burst her back 'to let loose in her death/a host of baby scorpions,' while uncle added "They're quite red at birth,/the little ones" ('A Minor Sacrifice').

In Ramanujan's poems, we get a unique representation of a typical Indian 'joint' family. John Jones writes about the Indian joint family system :

> It requires an ideal family, under the strong guidance of an ideal head, to live in peace and harmony under this system. Union is strength (Jones : 246).

Ramanujan realistically dwells upon the relative advantages of the 'extended' or 'joint' family system over the 'nuclear' family system. In highly complex and industrial societies, where the family performs minimal institutional functions, the nuclear family unit isolated from the wider kin group tends to predominate. The nuclear family, which is essentially 'urban' in nature, tends to be a mobile one, physically and socially, and it, therefore, tends towards a certain rootlessness. The sense of 'belonging,' born of living together for generations, which is a characteristic feature of an extended family, is absent or weak in a nuclear family. Ramanujan looks for extended connections in Indian past to recover the sense of 'belonging,' which would cure him, once for all, of his rootlessness. Thus, the recollections of Indian society would bring tranquillity to the hearts that 'make connection with alien veins,...beat/and learn to miss a beat in a foreign body.' ('Death and Good Citizen,' *Second Sight*).

WORKS CITED

Comfort, Alex. 1962. *Sex in Society*. Harmondsworth : Penguin.

Ezekiel, Nissim. 1989. *The Collected Poems*. New Delhi : Oxford University Press.

Hawkes, Terence. 1972. *Metaphor*. London : Methiuen.

Jha, Rama. 1981. "A Conversation with A.K. Ramanujan," *Humanities Review*, 3, 1 (Jan.-June) : 5-13.

Jones, John P. 1974. *India : Its Life and Thought*. New Delhi : Rave Books.

Naik, M.K. 1984. "A.K. Ramanujan and the Search for Roots," *Dimensions of Indian English Literature*. New Delhi : Sterling : 14-24.

Parthasarathy, R. (ed.). 1976. *Ten Twentieth-Century Indian Poets*. New Delhi : Oxford University Press.

Ramanujan, A.K. 1995. *The Collected Poems of A.K. Ramanujan* (ed.) Vinay Dharwadker. New Delhi : Oxford University Press. Referred to as *CP* in the text.

10

Roots that Roam : Relationships in Ramanujan's Poetry

—*PREMILA PAUL*

Indian Poetry in English has not yet managed to draw as much international attention and acclaim as contemporary Indian English Fiction. Some of the recent novelists have even eclipsed the importance of the earlier masters like 'the Big Three' — Mulk Raj Anand, Raja Rao and R.K. Narayan. But in the case of Indian Poetry in English, the reading public and the critics still swear by the older generation of poets — Nissim Ezekiel, A.K. Ramanujan, Jayanta Mahapatra and Kamala Das. The contribution made by each of these poets is unique and the importance and influence of these poets continue in the academic world.

Apart from being a major Indian poet in English, A.K. Ramanujan has been a sought after teacher of Dravidian Studies and Linguistics, South Asian Languages and Civilization and Anthropology. He is one of the very few poets who have made a great mark in the academic field as well. Another significant contribution made by him is his priceless translations of Tamil and Kannada literary texts into English. It is a special gift to the reading public in the multilingual India and beyond. Born of Tamil parents in Kannada-speaking Mysore, Ramanujan achieved competence in both the languages. He taught English Literature for a brief period in Quilon, Kerala. He married a Syrian Christian who familiarized him with Malayalam and Kerala culture. Language acquisition came naturally to him and soon he was well equipped to think and feel in several different languages. Gifted by nature and circumstances, Ramanujan remains an artist and translator par excellence.

As an artist who has taken adequate advantage of his multilingual and multicultural background, Ramanujan had no difficulty in making a success of himself in Western academia. He quickly gained recognition in both India and abroad. The crucial move to make a home of an alien land was a conscious choice. The contribution made by Ramanujan to South Asian Studies in various American Universities has been widely acclaimed. In 1976, he received the Padma Sri Award from the Government of India and in 1983 he received a Mac Arthur Fellowship. In 1990 he was elected to the American Academy of Arts and Sciences. But material success does not guarantee fulfillment, nor is it an insurance against the feeling of loss. As usual Ramanujan has made the best use of the neither-here-nor-there strider-like situation.

Expatriation is often thought of as a breach or a rift : as a break between the self and its home that is beyond repair. Yet we know that expatriation can also become a dynamic and enriching force in an individual. Ramanujan too feels this unhealable breach within him. The conducive work atmosphere and the sense of achievement at being a phenomenal success in an alien land cannot transform the United States into a home. But he senses it will remain a most satisfying workplace. However the constant awareness of this rift has given him the positive urges to create significant poetry. The title image of the striders in his very first volume of poetry pictures his own precarious poise. Straddling between cultures, poetry helps him make sense of this predicament and the conscious decision to live in it. Thus his expatriate status has become a boon to the literary world.

An extensive stay in the U.S. has also made Ramanujan realize what R. Parthasarathy writes in his 'Exile' :

> There is something to be said for exile :
> you learn roots are deep. (Parthasarathy : 15)

The more the poet lives and writes abroad, the more he becomes aware of his deep Indianness. Indianness is not merely a part of his past but what continues to live in him, condition and regulate his behaviour, attitudes and values. The poet proudly acknowledges the continued influence of the inherited value system and thereby affirms his deep and live relationship with people and places of the past. This is illustrated in his "Still Another View of Grace" :

> Bred Brahmin among singers of shivering hymns
> I shudder to the bone at hungers that roam the street
> beyond the constable's beat. (*CP* : 45)

Though ancestral strictures break down before the heat of sexual passion, they do so only after genuine attempts at resistance :

> ...Commandments crumbled
> in my father's past. Her tumbled hair suddenly known
> as silk in my angry hand, I shook a little
> and took her, behind the laws of my land. (*CP* : 45)

The approval and appreciation are still in favour of the inherited cultural and familial restraints.

Ramanujan's poetry deals with both individual and racial memory. Memory becomes a vital factor in keeping alive his relationship with India, within and without. It is more than a psychological prop or support. It is the very emotional base and creative spring board. To refer to memory as a major theme in Ramanujan's poetry in a way belittles its significance. It is not an object observed or experience analysed. Memory is the poet, his poetry is his memory, he writes on and of his memory. The act of remembering is not a dull cud chewing of the past: it brings alive all in his past that is usable. It is not a kind of sentimental nostalgia that hampers progress and refuses to see any good in the here and the now. It is an active lingering to leap forward with vigour. An active memory helps to establish rootedness. The awareness and assurance of rootedness in turn establishes emotional stability and enables him to integrate the past and the present, the immediate and the remote, all that is within and without, the Western work-orientedness and the Indian human-relatedness. Most of his work in the U.S. is related to his roots in India — Dravidian Linguistics, anthropology and translation of Indian literary texts. His primary agenda is not to interpret or promote his exotic "Hindoo India" to an alien audience. It is a simple act of being true to himself and his relatedness from which he derives sustenance. It is also an act of homage to his Indian heritage. Every poem bears testimony to the presence of the past, the vital relationship with people, with family, culture, language and country.

Many of the poems in the volume, *Relations*, focus on his individual relationships and their lasting effect on his poetic consciousness. Some of them assert and glorify his relationship with the immediate family members. The mental image of the old mother picking up a grain of rice from the kitchen floor turns on his memory of his mother in different stages — "the silk and white petal" of her youth, her running back "from rain to the crying cradles," and then her wrinkled hands in old age like a "wet eagle's." A string of visual images, like the three diamonds in her ear rings splashing a handful of needles and her saree hanging loose like "feather of a one time wing" whirl in his consciousness. These striking poetic images reveal his controlled grief and deep love for the mother though there is no direct reference to her deformity or his nostalgia :

My cold parchment tongue licks bark
in the mouth when I see her four
still sensible fingers slowly flex
to pick a grain of rice from the kitchen floor.

(*CP* : 61)

The presence of the absent father is felt intensely in "Obituary." The poet adopts a mock-ironic tone and lists the unfinished tasks, the rites and the legacy of responsibilities left behind by the father. Here again he effectively underplays the poignancy of grief. In the last three stanzas, in a single sentence he maintains artistic detachment by his striking use of images of impersonal shopping. The final result of the father's death is that

....he left us
a changed mother
and more than
one annual ritual. (*CP* : 112)

"Snakes" is a significant poem that shifts from the rural Indian locale to the urban Western background, and *vice-versa*.

By combining the real and the dream experience, the poet suggests the need to confront real and imagined fear. There are vignettes of memory of home and family, of mother giving milk to snakes in saucers, and the snake man looking "for father's smiling money." Precise, vivid, concrete images build up the panic. In a state of paranoia, the sister's knee-long braid held by a score of clean new pins reminds him of the scales of a snake. Images of family members are evoked now and then even while dealing with an abstract feeling.

Memory plays a special creative role in the poem, "Looking for a Cousin on a Swing." It is not a mere recollection of an event. It is a childhood experience viewed, analysed and assessed from an adult perspective. The poem deals with the first intimations of sexuality by means of the deft use of the swing image. The cousin's initiation from innocence to awareness of the libidinous self is presented with deliberate dubiousness. The poem abounds in images of erotic suggestion, so that even a sneeze could mean an explosion of passion at the slightest provocation.

"Love Poem for a Wife-I" tries to analyse the cause of the emotional rift between the persona and his wife, and attributes the lack of a feeling of emotional oneness to an unshared childhood. What makes this poem different from other poetic recollections is that its attempt consciously to enter another's past reveals with utter clarity the limits of the existing relationship with that person. "Love Poem for a Wife-I" shows that the desire to enter another's life inevitably ends in frustration. The poem records nostalgic recollections of both his and his wife's past. The images in a wedding picture of his father wearing a turban and his mother wearing silver rings on her second toe, or his father's noisy bathing habit of slapping soap on his back are as important as the image of the wife's anxious father, cigaratte in hand, pacing to the fro, awaiting the daughter's late return after what she thought "was an innocent/date with a nice Muslim friend/who only hinted at touches." The wife's attempt to reconstruct her childhood with the help of her brother James, each claiming the reliability of one's own memory, leaves him and James' wife total outsiders. The persona realizes that total emotional understanding between husband and wife is impossible to achieve unless they "carry marriage back into/the namelessness of childhoods." The tone shows a longing for the impossible, for the presence of absent people and places, and a desire to replenish emotional springs with new relationships.

Though individual family members are mentioned in it, it is 'family' as an institution that is glorified in "Small-scale Reflections on a Great House." The carefully worked out imprecision of the poem, images extended, crowded yet telling details and some even unnecessary, deft repetitions and deliberate digressions suggest the ever enlarging family, the composition of which is as vague as the relationships. The relationships, however vague and distant they may be, are important, and therefore each person is sure of his or her respective slot in the family institution. This poem seems to endorse the Frostian idea that

> Home is the place where, when you have to go there,
> They have to take you in.
>
> ('The Death of the Hired Man,' Frost : 165)

Every component/person could lose his or her individual identity or make up for the lack of it and take on the familial identity. Ramanujan's poem gives a long catalogue of such possibilities.

Such a great house could also stand for the ancient house of Hindu heritage that absorbs from time to time various elements, but attempts to make of them a beautiful synthesis. It also could stand for the poet's own storehouse of memory, retaining, nurturing and designating anything/any one that strays into it. The poem lists the ordinary, day-to-day events in the Great House in a semi-humorous manner, only to end the list with two out of the ordinary occurrences that envelope the Great House in gloom. The poem is also a tribute to the great tradition of a large joint family. But it is, more than anything else, concerned with the crowded memories that will never leave the poet, relationships that he would never let go, the ones that make up a family and sustain him wherever he may be.

Even a poem like, "A River" that does not focus on a familial motif reveals his obsession with memory and relationships. The poem is born out of the memory of his Madurai visit, when the floods made of the River Vaigai a real river. Here, the poet contrasts images of drought and floods. His complaint is that contemporary poets do not see poetic possibilities in human situations. Instead, they seek stock poetic subjects or sing of past glories. Even when faced with a disturbing situation they become literal minded, unmindful of human concerns. Ramanujan locates this poem in Madurai, the seat of ancient Tamil culture and Sangam Literature. He uses grim images to suggest the emotional drought and artistic aridity in contemporary Tamil poetry, a contrast to the rich surge of old Sangam Poetry.

"Conventions of Despair" shows how the poet is bound to remain a downright conventional Indian. Ramanujan does not decry what is considered Western culture. Nor does he blindly venerate everything that is considered Indian. But still it is impossible for him to adopt modern ways of coming to terms with despair.

> ...I cannot unlearn
> conventions of despair.
> They have their pride.
> I must seek and will find
> my particular hell only in my hindu mind :... (*CP* : 34)

The modern prescriptions for dealing with despair have no appeal to him. The inherent culture of a person is known only by the way he/she comes to terms with grief. The in-built safety guards and the survival strategies picked up in the formative years alone may come to rescue.

Finally, it is the rootedness in one's own culture and the relatedness to one's family and people that offer emotional stability to Ramanujan. The assurance of this basic relationship has enabled him to successfully connect himself to the outside world. The values of acceptance and accommodation inherited from the culture of the Great House have helped him to open his doors and himself to others and other cultures. The expatriate in him would never let Western work-orientedness subordinate the importance of relationships. Ironically that is the secret of his remarkable success in his work in the United States. Focus on work and fulfilment in work are possible only when priorities are clear and straight.

Even the relationship with those who are dead is not irrelevant. With the help of an active memory, the past is activised, and interaction between the past and the present continues. Real events of the past come processed, bearing new meaning for the present. Memory helps to retrieve details, reinterpret them, rearrange them for the better understanding of the present. There is no lack or fear of a loss of connection as long as there is memory. The poet thus lives in both the worlds — inner and outer — both equally vivid and vital. Memory makes the co-existence and integration of both worlds possible, provides impetus for work and progress, and in these ways enables the artist to 'see life steadily' and to 'see it whole.'

WORKS CITED

Frost, Robert. 1946. *Robert Frost's Poems* (ed.) Louis Untermeyer. New York : Washington Square Press.

Parthasarathy, R. 1977. *Rough Passage*, Delhi : Oxford.

Ramanujan, A.K. 1995. *The Collected Poems of A.K. Ramanujan* (ed.) Vinay Dharwadker. New Delhi : Oxford. Referred of as *CP* in the text.

11

Some Interesting Structural Features of A.K. Ramanujan's Poetry

—SHIRISH V. CHINDHADE

Like Arundhati Roy's novel *The God of Small Things,* A.K. Ramanujan's poetry, too, is a celebration of the small things of life with the main difference that Roy's expression is one of an inebriated abandon, a spontaneous overflow of powerful feelings, while Ramanujan's method is one of ruthless self-restraint which may be because, unlike Roy, he sets out to go naked in the world, that is, without adopting a mask. Therefore, an observable measure of embarrassment oppresses him as the poetry he writes is too personal, rising from his own life and experiences and so throwing the poet into confusion as to how much to let out and how much to withhold. But, then, it is a facile observation that because of this intruding and obtrusive presence of the private person, the recurring concerns in Ramanujan's poetry get confined to only a few but well-defined ones with subtle overlaps. They are : familial situations and relations, the American experience and memories of home, the Hindu classics, mythology and traditions, fear and anxiety, self-search and self-definition, and the inextricable inter-relatedness of birth and death. In other words, every Ramanujan poem has a subtext, and whatever the theme of a poem, the subtext is A.K. Ramanujan himself, roping in the kith and the kin, the flora and the fauna, the past and the memories anchored to it and the incidents and situations he himself has been an eye-witness to and participated in. During the process of re-living these experiences the poet's main strategy is one of taciturnity. That is to say, things happen to him; he doesn't cause them to happen. As a participant he resists commenting; he notes the comments of those who offer them. Consequently, when it comes to communicate and comment as a poet he is on his guard, most terse, laconic, self-effacing, almost unwilling to speak, lest, he is afraid, he should divulge a secret, break a confidence and thus invite public opprobrium at himself and his people. So he would rather half speak and half suppress; and so his poetry hides more than it reveals. His catalogue of fears, for instance, among many other things includes :

> And now, at thirty-nine, to the old fear
> of depths and heights,
> Of father in the bedroom...
>
> ('Entries for a Catalogue of Fears,' *CP* : 86)

And then he veers off to other things, Or, in "Small-scale Reflections on a Great House" the sudden memory sends a flash :

> lame wandering cows from nowhere
> have been known to be tethered,
> given a name, encouraged
>
> to get pregnant in the broad daylight
> of the street under the elders'
> supervision, the girls hiding
> behind windows with holes in them. (*CP* : 96)

Or, digging into his own ancestry this is what he has to say about his grandmother :

> my one true ancestor,
> the fisherman lover who waylaid her
> in the ropes in the Madras harbour
> took her often from behind
> imprinting on her face and body...
> lasting impression of his net. (*CP* : 62)

Thus in poem after poem a personal, familial secret is divulged, and like cough and love, the more it is suppressed, the more powerfully it erupts. And what is surprising is the ordinariness of the material, the experience; but the poet has mastered the alchemy that metamorphoses the casual into the crucial which resultantly affords a great deal of joy of recognition. Thus is made the interior landscape a public promenade. Is it a case of distant views being enchanting due to the poet's self-exile in America? In other words, the poet is permanently stressed out — blocked up like an old crypt, as Pinter's Martin Luther says at one place. The poetry is the expression of this stress, of an existential tension which imposes a staccato effect on the utterances. It is as though, the poet is deliberately giving out the impression that he hums and haws, stammers and stutters, fumbles and falters because soon he is going to commit felony of infidelity to the family.

In addition to this personal/familial inhibitory factor, there may be a few others also that encourage a reluctance to speak, giving the poetry certain characteristic structural features. This requires us to look for what comes from where, that is, the sources and influences operating in his poetry. Ramanujan partly shares this information with us : "English and my disciplines (linguistics, anthropology) give me my "outer" forms — linguistic, metrical, logical and other such ways of shaping experience; and my first thirty years in India, my frequent visits and fieldtrips, my personal and professional preoccupations with Kannada, Tamil, the classics and folklore give me my substance, my 'inner' forms, images and symbols. They are continuous with each other, and I no longer can tell what comes from where" (Cited in Parthasarathy, *Ten* : 96).

The classics referred to here are certainly the Sanskrit ones from which rise the Tamil classics too, all imposing their "agglutinative touch" (Parthasarathy, *Rough* : 47) to Ramanujan's English, a language already characterised by its inherent conciseness. The influences are wide-ranging from the East to the West. Among the Western ones are the English metaphysical poets, George Herbert, Keats, Lawrence and mainly the American William Carlos Williams, not to mention Ramanujan's vast acquaintance with world literatures (Jha : IiI). The influence of Williams may be operating in two ways : Williams believed that poetry is inherent in the little things of the word and, secondly, he liked to present an object without further comment, which comes close to the Imagist mode. A short poem like

"The Striders" evidences the traces of the first kind of impact. On the first reading of the poem one is despaired by its flimsy, inconsequential content, just "eye-deep." This is reinforced by the plathoric use of nouns and adjectives of delicacy and diminution such as thin-stemmed, bubble-eyed, bugs, capillary legs, weightless, ripple skin, landslide of light and tiny. However, the poem unfolds its dramatic effect mainly through irony and allusion. Irony helps to juxtapose the tiny insect with prophets walking on water, while the prophets themselves allude to both Indian and Christian myths, thus universalising the experience. The drama is significantly adumbrated by opening the poem with the conjunction 'and, Ramanujan's favourite gimmick of beginning the narration *in medias res*.

"The Striders" reminds of Lawrence's "Mosquito" which dramatises a trial of strength between man and mosquito :

> Come then, let us play at unawares,
> And see who wins in this sly game of bluff —
> Man or mosquito. (Hewett : 193)

The resemblance goes beyond the level of the tonic to become metaphor and symbol. The mosquito is symbolically an atom that has an incalculable energy-store at its nucleus and can destroy the whole humanity, while the striders are metaphorically prophets who perform miracles to save humanity. And yet, Ramanujan's is a better poem because it offers a representative model of poetry that tells us what to look for in a Ramanujan poem, both thematically and structurally. The poem, thus, appropriately opens the poet's very first collection with the same name. It is in this sense a "major" poem, as Roomy Naqui claims (Naqui : 193).

One very recurring and favourite expressive mode of Ramanujan is the fictive one. He likes to set out with a tale to narrate, a situation to delineate, an incident to dramatise, every time rummaging in the storehouse of his personal memories, but he always sees to it that he makes the long story short. That is a compulsive behaviour with him, as pointed out above. The proportions are not epic and the narration is summary, as if he is in a great hurry to finish it off and have done with it at the earliest since it is embarrassing to make it public. This results in snappy lines, half expressions, short stanzas, elipsis, and only a couple of sentences, sometimes even only one sentence in which to wind up a poem, often using the Miltonic technique of starting a poem with the middle brought forward.

The one-sentence poem is Ramanujan's forte, which helps him to achieve a speedy, precise and concise narration. And even if a poem demands a longer space, the number of sentences is under strict control, to the minimum. "Small-scale Reflections on a Great House" (*CP* : 96-99) has ninety-one lines with only ten sentences but a whole exciting family history unfolds fast, punctuated with humour and irony and, on a sudden, coming to a dead (full-) stop most dramatically and unexpectedly, that is, with an unexpected conclusion, and, as often, with a standoffish single punch-line. "Looking for a Cousin on a Swing" (*CP* : 19) unfolds the whole history of a calf love in just twenty-three lines in two sentences only. As usual, the last punch line stands by itself, "if someone suddenly sneezed." Innocence and experience are juxtaposed highlighting each other. The act of someone suddenly sneezing opens up a whole cluster of suggestions of fear, suspicion, surprise, memory in a flash, and a world permanently lost, all in a susurrus of alliteration of "s" sound softened by the nasal "n". A similar impact is achieved in "A River" (*CP* : 38-39) also in the concluding single line "to tell them apart" offering a severe comment on repetitive (Tamil) literature that fails to grapple with the bare facts of life and thus comes still-born like the identical twins in the poem.

"Breaded Fish" (*CP* : 7) and "Still Life" (*CP* : 12), two memory poems of love, are typically short and graphic in the presentation of experience, talking humbly about fishes, women and lovers. "Breaded Fish" is rhymed with an unusual scheme of aab, ccb, aab, aab, written in the recurrent triplet stanza form, consisting of only two sentences. The first full stop comes almost after eleven and a quarter lines and then follows the concluding line making a total of twelve lines with four stanzas of one triplet each, unfolding a rather gruesome, unhappy tale. Two dissimilar, unconnected incidents light up each other; both belong to the past; both are sad : a woman, the wife, lovingly thrusting a breaded fish into the poet's mouth. The fish smells obnoxiously, opening the hood memory in his mind of the dead body of a woman rolled to the shore by the ebb, breaded by sand. The poet's heart beats in his mouth. Both the experiences leave a bad taste in the mouth.

"Still Life" is even shorter, consisting of eleven lines with the first full stop coming in the third line after eleven words. Here also memory works through association : the half-eaten sandwich, bread, carrying the shape of her bite after the woman has left a while ago. This is a technique learned from William Carlos Williams whereby an object is presented without further comment. Compare this for its picturesque presentation with a few lines of "The Wake" by the American poet Rita Dove :

> But the rooms still gaped —
> The green hanger swang empty, and
> The head of the table
> Demanded a plate. (Dove : 4)

Since Ramanujan's poems invariably have a subtext — Ramanujan himself — the self sometimes tries to assert itself in a desperate self-search. As a rule, a celebrated short poem like "Self-Portrait" (*CP* : 23) appears at different stages of time in other companion pieces like "Extended Family" (*CP* : 169) and "Not Knowing" (*CP* : 216). Typically, "Self-Portrait" has a single sentence spread in nine short lines, concluding that the portrait has been signed in a corner by his father[1]. There is a liberal use of eye-rhymes and assonance like, everyone/unknown; shop-windows/lawa; stranger/corner/father, suggesting links in the lineage. It opens with "I" and ends with "father," two terminal points containing, as it were, the entire genealogy ("I resemble everyone"). But in a subtle way it also tells us that he has no identity of his own, independent of his family, an engagement recurrent in Ramanujan's poetry. The same message is conveyed

1. Girish Karnad aptly explains how a single, simple phrase throws up multiple suggestions : "The plural in 'Shop Windows' is significant. A self-portrait is made up of multiple reflections. Ramanujan played various roles in his life, a poet in Kannada and English, Tamil Scholar, anthropologist, linguist and translator..." This reading is reinforced in the line "I resemble everyone." — "The Poems of Pain," *Indian Express*, 3 Aug. 1995, p. 4.

in "Extended Family" which opens with "grandfather" and concludes with "great-grandson" yet to come. In between, again, stands the whole lineage covered in forty-seven lines without a full stop, suggesting the continuity further beyond.

The self-definition and self-search painfully intensify in "Not Knowing" which is a recent poem included in the last collection *The Black Hen*. Trying to know oneself proves to be a confusing and shattering experience as it fails every time :

> till mirrors in a mirror shop
> break me up into how many I was
> show me in profile and fragment... (*CP* : 216)

Keki Daruwalla observes, "Through the landscape of his poetry Ramanujan seems to be carrying on two kinds of conversation with himself — not just the interior monologue or dialogue, but also mirror-talk; a mirror-talk that turns things askew, as if epiphany and self-revelation are passing through a cubist's prism. If distorted reality is reality in fact, then this is how, I suppose, one would go about it" (Daruwalla : 34). Akshay Kumar notes Ramanujan's use of parody to achieve the same effect, *i.e.*, through it "the self is continually reviewed and deconstructed" (Kumar : 10).

The sonnet form has frequently attracted Ramanujan, though he often tends to produce a near sonnet or sometimes what Hopkins called "curtal" (curtailed) sonnet. The stanzaic division of 4+4+3+3 is often preferred without any rigidly regular rhyme scheme. "Routine Day Sonnet" (*CP* : 68) has surprising effects with its rhyme scheme aa, bb, cc, aa (that forms the octave with 4+4 lines), ddd, eee. The rather undramatic, sleepy routine in the house spills over the octave making the householder restless; something is amiss : "A bullock cart/in an Eskimo dream." However, this lax routine is suddenly shattered as though he was sleeping on the crater of a dormant volcano. The volley of insults, the fusillade of abuses is fired by the hysteric wife in the middle of the quiet night. — And that itself is a routine day occurrence! The rhymes of the sestet slyly reflect the routine; that's where the poet's technical triumph lies.

Like the theme of self-search explored in these three poems spanning several years of the poet's life, another poetic "trilogy" deals with a common theme : the mystery of poetic creation. Writing poetry for Ramanujan is neither an escape from personality nor an escape into personality (though he has a personality of his own as a poet) to borrow T.S. Eliot's famous phrase. It is an experience, an act of "putting together and pulling apart" as Molly Daniels puts it (*CP* : 279). It is painful, devastating, shattering and constructive, thus uniting contraries. The three poems that analyse this experience are, "The Death of a Poem" (*CP* : 142), "The Black Hen" (*CP* : 195) and "No Fifth Man" (*CP* : 243). Destruction and creation, death and birth are two sides of the same coin and they are present in the act of making a poem, creating a work of art. "The Death of a Poem" is deceptive in many ways : its brevity (three stanzas of three lines each, totally employing only fourteen words!), its play on words, its extended metaphor, its (light) tone, its common diction, its courtroom drama and its images. The common knowledge that poetry is a construct of images is conveyed metaphorically, the conscience-stricken jury/judge being the poet himself. By further extension, is the jury Ramanujan himself, as he has chosen to construct poetry mainly not in his own language but in an alien, acquired one? Bruce King has a scholarly comment to offer; "In contemporary literary theory, a narrative is seen as a continual delaying of a conclusion which completes the structure. Moreover, the shift from the image as gesture seems to be a part of a larger recent cultural movement in which the relationship between form and meaning is called into question. In this situation, language, especially language structures, are external and temporal" (King : 84).

"The Black Hen," one of the most recent of Ramanujan's poems, as masterly as all his work (—"stitch by stitch") is about making a poem, which after completed mortally frightens the maker. It belongs to the group of last poems that were found in Ramanujan's computer just before his death. It is a poem "that makes the flesh creep," says Adil Jussawalla. "In giving life to the poem the poet has simultaneously created an emblem for his own death" (Jussawalla). And if this curtal sonnet (thirteen lines) is not minatory are premonitory enough in tone, then we have to read the third poem in the set, "No Fifth Man."

It starts in *medias res* to reinterpret an old Sanskrit parable from Vishnusharma's celebrated *Panchatantra*. The parable narrates how four learned Brahmins who knew the miraculous *Sanjivani Vidya* that breathes life into dead creatures, use it to resuscitate a dead tiger that, in turn, devours them all, flesh and bone. Their fifth friend, an ignoramous, illiterate oaf, climbs up a tree before the mantra is cast on the dead tiger. He is save! Ramanujan equates the making of a poem with the using of the *Sanjivani Vidya* and concludes :

> poetry too is a tigress,
> except there's no fifth
> man left on a tree
> when she takes your breath
> away.

Again, the same preoccupation with the unified operation of contraries is reinforced and reiterated here. In all these cases he uses irony to mark the contraries.

Like his thematic engagements, Ramanujan's poetic techniques, devices and structures are also limited and recurrent. They show a consistency throughout his poetic career. The promises of subtle suggestions, masterful methods, oblique allusions made in the early poem, "The Striders" are all ably kept in the poems in *The Black Hen* published posthumously in the *Collected Poems*. Indeed, they hold further promise of even more mature work. The promise, however, remained unfulfilled due to Ramanujan's sudden, premature death in 1993. But so much of quality work is already offered that only an extended and continuous assessment can fully open up the "cave of Ali Baba!"

To read Ramanujan is to start delving into a mine of gold, as he loads every rift with ore!

WORKS CITED

Daruwalla, Keki N. 1995. "Gorging Contraries" *The Book Review,* 19, 8 (Aug.) 33-34.

Dove, Rita. 1994. "The Wake" *Spán*, 3 (March) : 4.

Hewett, R.P. (ed). 1969. *A Choice of Poets.* London : Harrap.

Jha, Rama. 1980. "Between Two Worlds," "*Times of India*, 20 Jan. : III.

Jussawalla, Adil. Not dated. "By the Way," *Times of India*.

King, Bruce. 1991. *Three Indian Poets.* Madras : Oxford University Press.

Kumar, Akshay. 1998."Parody as Subfurfuge : Cultural Politics of A.K. Ramanujan's Poetry," *New Quest*, 127 (Jan.-Feb.) : 10.

Naqui, Roomy. 1996. "A Poetics of Space," *Indian Literature*, 173, 39 (May-June) : 193.

Parthasarathy, R. 1976. *Rough Passage*. New Delhi : Oxford University Press.

—— (ed.). 1976. *Ten Twentieth-Century Indian Poets*. New Delhi : Oxford University Press.

Ramanujan, A.K. 1995. *The Collected Poems of A.K. Ramanujan* (ed.) Vinay Dharwadker. New Delhi : Oxford University Press. Refered to as *CP* in the text.

12

The Black Hen : A Trans-Continental Experience

—*P.K. KALYANI*

Discussing culture and globalization at the end of the millennium, one may very well agree with Paul Rabinow :

> When a culture stops moving, when its structures of belief no longer offer a means to integrate, create and make meaningful new experiences, then a process of alienation begins. Tradition is opposed not to modernity but to alienation (Rabinow : 11).

It is a similar view that is presented by Gareth Griffith in his essay "Culture and Identity : Politics and Writing in Some Recent Post-Colonial Texts" :

> ....cultural encounters in post-colonial societies involve a mutuality, in which the categories of oppressor and oppressed are bound together in what Harris terms as a mutual erosion of bias. The result is the dismissal of fixed and dead categories of history, or the freezing of specific moments of the ongoing historical dialectic into new universal and historical reality (Griffith : 441).

The mutual erosion of bias, which Griffith speaks of, leads to a syncraticity that is

> neither a threat to identity nor a denial of the uniqueness of post-colonial reality. Instead texts which embrace the complex and syncratic nature of post-colonial world inevitably end by questioning both a cultural politics which seeks to incorporate the post-colonial world back into some new universal and Eurocentric paradigm and that

> which seeks simply to reconstitute the local and traditional outside a very conscious awareness of historical change and present political realities (Griffith : 443).

It becomes clear then, from the words of those culture critics that the culture bound activities in the post colonial context need not be hegemonic in one way or other in that the centre of the hegemony now shifts from the colonies to the colonized or to the new universal/global. In other words, as Griffith says :

> In effect we are all in each other's backyard. Hence, on paradoxical consequence of the process of globalization, the awareness of the finitude and the boundedness of the planet and humanity, is not to produce homogeneity but to familiarize us with greater diversity, the extensive range of local cultures (Griffith : 437).

In this paper I intend to examine the syncraticity of cultures that A.K. Ramanujan has made in his posthumous collection of poems titled *The Black Hen*. It then becomes essential to explain what I mean by trans-continental. The poems in this collection not only cut through/across but also beyond the Indian subcontinent on the cultural plain. In his poems what one traces is the perception of not only the Indian but of varied other countries as well, that lie between Chicago on the West and Japan on the East. Ramanujan is an Indian poet who wrote in Kannada, translated classical Tamil poetry, was thorough in his knowledge of Indian folklore, myths and classics and also wrote in English his experiences. There is therefore a syncraticity of the assorted Indian itself in the poet. Widely travelled and read, and based in Chicao his experience gained one more shade that extends beyond the boundaries of the Indian subcontinent. In *The Black Hen* one could observe the portrayal of these wide experiences that overflow the subcontinental boundaries through places like Chicago, Yukon, Japan and China. In doing so he is concerned with human relationships, culture, nature and Time as in his earlier three collections of poems. Writing an Introduction to the posthumously published *The Collected Poems of A.K. Ramanujan* Vinay Dharwadker traces the major trends of thoughts that influenced Ramanujan as the Virashaiva tradition in Kannada, Srivaishnava tradition in Tamil, Spinoza's philosophy, Zen Buddhism, and the philosophy of Pascal and that of Borges. Besides these philosophical thoughts his knowledge relating to the natural world, cultures of various places and human body as well as his conception of time find a place in these poems. To put it in a nutshell, Ramanujan is involved in "mapping the mutual interdependencies of body, nature, culture and time until they cover an immense span of human and natural history" (*CP* : 27).

The present study has taken the poems which relate to the topic and has made individual analysis of them. The first section discusses the theory used and introduces the poet from the point of view of the study. The second section is the analysis of the poems. The third section summarizes the discussion in the attempt to establish the hypothesis.

The very first poem in the collection taken for the study, the title-piece 'The Black Hen' knits the artists all over the world together through the imagery of embroidery. He is of the firm view that if poetry does not come as naturally as the leaves come to a tree then it better not come at all. However, he is aware that it does come sometimes in a strained manner, consciously written by the poet; and if it does come so by the careful and conscious working of the poet, then the beauty of the poem is lost and the poem becomes devoid of the aesthetic and would resemble a carefully embroidered black hen with its red eyes staring at the embroiderer :

> yet it comes sometimes
> as the black hen
> with a red round eye
> on the embroidery
> stitch by stitch
> dropped and found again
>
> ... ...
>
> the black hen stares
> with its round red eye
> and you're afraid. (*CP* : 195)

The rural countryside is represented by the black hen; and the picturesque description of the embroidered hen symbolically scares the reader of the strained writing and also takes one back in times to a different, now almost extinct, atmosphere of the grandmother's time when there was time for rearing hen at the backyard and embroidery. In the poem there is a contrasting of the past and the present, the urban and the rural as well as the aesthetic natural and the cultivated artificial brought into effect by a contrastive voice and silence.

The second poem titled 'Foundlings of the Yukon' (*CP* : 196-97) has a broader canvass. The poem takes the reader across not only the continents but also across a vast span of time to the ancient civilization of the Pleistocene times, unlike in the previous poem where the time gap is only a generation or two wide. The Yukon valley is temporally and spatially in the farthest corner of the map. The civilization that has been buried by a landslide is not dead. It is alive, ten thousand years after. The seeds that were buried and discovered extend their warmth in just forty eight hours. These "upstarts" are unlike the Alaskan lupine that takes about three years to boom. These sprouts are warm and friendly and

> ... ...hasty
> for birth and seasons, for names,
> genes, for passing on...,

like man who is eager to have his genes passed on to his progeny. Further, the quick sprouting of the buried seeds is

compared to the racial memory of man :

> ... ... the kick
> and shift of an intra uterine
> memory.

and to the

> ... ... pent-up
> centenarian's sudden burst
> of lust...

They are also compared to the *Duino Elegies* of Rainer Maria Rilke in which the seeds of modernism lie embedded :

... ... may be
just elegies in the Duino unbound
From the dark, ...

This poem linkes Time, continents, nature, literature and literary movement.

The poem titled 'Shadows' (*CP* : 199) opens with an observation that is applicable to all people irrespective of time and space :

Shadows fall between people
when they walk in the sun.

The second stanza with its reference to men who 'explode stepping on mines' takes one closer to the land mines of the North African countries. From the African continent the reader is given a ritual lift to the Indian subcontinent, where under the patriarchal system boy children are preferred to girl children and to beget the boy child certain practices are followed :

Women circumambulate the peepul
tree hoping for a son.

If the circumambulation does not grant the boy child, then the girl child that is born will have to live in Shadows :

Daughters breed in stark
family dungeons like slow
perrennials waiting for the rains.

From the Indian subcontinent the reader is lifted to Europe where

War heroes return in special trains
covered with blood and flags. They blow
bugles at home, brawl in pubs, and bark
orders at dogs, kill and flay twenty-one
nurses and hang one from a maple.

The poem 'At Zero' (*CP* : 200-01) speaks how at zero hour there is a standstill universally. However, in the poem there is a slant towards the Indian, with the couple of references to Indian customs. The first reference is to the brahmin widowhood. Indian women when they become widows are forced to live a plain life in the sense that they are not to use any coloured dresses or decorations. The woman who used to decorate herself with kumkum, flowers, ornaments and silk so elaborately till yesterday is shaved of her tresses and is made to wear white. The stillness of the zero hour is compared to the blankness/stillness of life of the Brahmin widow. Further, towards the end of the poem, there is the reference to the story of the potter saint, who in the ecstasy of worshipping his lord, Shiva, tramples upon his child to death :

> at zero, as when the potter-saint
> singing hymns, dancing
> his god, kneeded with his feet
> the soft red clay, burying
> alive his youngest child.

Like at the zero hour when all the movements come to an end and there is a stoppage of passing time, in the saints mind at the moment of worship there is only ecstasy and no other thoughts, emotions and consciousness.

In 'Salamanders' (*CP* : 202-03) the poet finds a link between man and the salamanders. The salamanders eat fire but are born in slushes in the woods after the rain. According to Ramanujan, man is no different from these salamanders :

> We, denizens of this nowhere nothing,
> flame within black flame, where red
> marries green and annuls it in the act,
> yellow shade in yellow shadow, empty hub
> of the turning wheel, mother and father
>
> of the forever unborn, obeying edicts
> written in smoke by war for countries
> that never were — we, we burn
> and eat fire no less than salamanders
>
> but live in the wet, crawl in the slush,
> five-toed lizards eating dragonflies,
> waiting no less than the three-toed for a turn
> of the body's season to copulate and people
> the woods with babies satin to the eye
>
> and velvet to the touch...

Man who is very much like the lizards in their habitat and living, can be surprising only to the "Hollywood aliens who know us only/through legends or medieval woodcuts." There is a quick peep into the Hollywood world where Aliens are created and they are so life-like that the poet's irony sees the real as the legend or cut out, from the Hollywood-Alien's point of view.

'Traces' (*CP* : 204) contains legends that are Indian. Speaking of the distance between the earth and the constellation, the poet says that 'only to an eye,' they are light years away. For the Indian, on the contrary, they are very close to their life — every day life.

> ... ... on the earth
> that reads its fate in the Seven
> Sages and the Milky Way

The influence of the milky way and the constellation of the Sapta Rishi are so closely intertwined with the life for the Indian that, all that happened in ones life is explained with a reading of the stars.

Not only the influence of the stars is felt on the life of an Indian, but the influence of the oceans is also felt. The difference in the context is that all people feel the influence of the oceans. The traces that oceans leave on life are not limited to the creation of not only

> ... ... shores, beaches, marinas,
> vacations, continents, harbors,
> ships and submarines, undersea
> kingdoms, whale song, moontides

but also literature :

> The Tempest, Moby Dick,
> and Robinson Crusoe.

which transport minds to different literary shores across the oceans.

If 'Fire' (*CP* : 205) levels down Simla and Calfornia by the 'Super-natural fire' prodding one to think of the two places separated by oceans, 'Birthdays' (*CP* : 206-07). fraternizes people of different places. St. Francis of Assissi, Shakespeare, Gandhi and Washington have all their birthdays marked on the calendars and celebrated nationally. But so are inventions, institutions and trees that recycle the seasons. Birthdays level down differences between men, man and materials as well as man and nature. In uniting man with nature death goes one step further :

> but death? Is it dispersal
> of gathered energies
> back into their elements
> earth, air, water and fire,
> a reworking into other moulds,
> grass, worm, bacterial glow
> lights, and mother-matter
> for other off-spring with names
> and forms clocked into seasons?

"Fog" (*CP* : 208) takes the reader from the rural to the urban scene. The regular movement of the eye that has been pinned to the desire to move is compared to the oxen driven oil press that can be traced to the villages of a couple of generations ago. In the second stanza the reader is taken to the claustrophobic elevators in the city. In the city, the trees that sway with green leaves are substituted by 'a labyrinth with cement pillars/trees without leaf or season.'

'One More On A Deathless Theme' (*CP* : 209-11) is yet another poem that links man with nature. First, the poet compares the body that will one day be short of breath to a dog who 'will be buried with an apple tree/planted on her to burst/into blossom in April/to be eaten as a red-green apple.' After death :

> Every one in this street
> will become cold, lie under stones
> or be scattered as ash
> in rivers and oceans.

Death traces man's relationship with the flora and the fauna. The poet's wife makes him a 'God whose one Half/is Woman.' This of course refers to the Ardhanari shwar concept in Hindu mythology. Lord Shiva accepted his consort Parvati as the oneself of his energy/body and hence the name Ardhanari which means one half is women.

In the same poem relationships extend to outer space as well. The poet who imagines his return to life after death compares himself to the astronauts who return from 'far away

Jupiters.' When they return from unknown places every form of life — trees as well as insects and animals would wait for them. Similarly the poet hopes that they would wait for him also when he returns after death :

would be forever there
waiting for me
as they 've always done
for astronauts any time they return
from farway Jupiters
or just downtown.

In 'August' (*CP* : 212-13) there are two images which the poet uses to explain how the annual calender

> constructed empirically and rationally can be recast as the cyclical chronology of the anniversaries of the births and deaths, quarrels, marriages and divorces in the history of one extended family. That is, an objective measure of time can be replaced by and become indistinguishable...from a completely subjective accounting of days, months and years (*CP* : 27).

The warmth of the couple of months is compared to grandmother's brewed coffee :

The next three months
were tepid like the coffee
in grandmother's village house.

The persisting heat of April to June is compared to the persistance of the prayer :

April to June turned
night and day like
a temple lamp kept alive
by a cripple praying
for her legs...

The poem 'On Not Learning From Animals' (*CP* : 217) begins with a positive note, emphasising the need to learn from animals. They are honest and not hypocrites like man. Nothing really disturbs them for they practice detachment in attachment.

... ... cats
sleep through a war, Dogs ignore your sister's

cancer, forgive betrayals and rations,
while all morning a man cannot bear his own
betrayal after sleeping with two women.
But a dog will not mount one bitch after
another nor want to kill himself
for being a cad :
... ... and quails are monogamous
says the encyclopeaedia. The baboon
has a harem but he is not tormented
by claims for equal time.

The ironical twist comes in the last few lines when the speaker realises that situations are not so different in the animal world as well when it comes to patriarchal values :

a female ape with a black striped snout
sort out patiently with her long hands, then
sniff, and lick lettuce leaves clean for her lord
and master while he growled all through (*CP* : 217)

The three poems titled 'Mythologies I' (*CP* : 221), 'Mythologies II' (*CP* : 226) and 'Mythologies III' (*CP* : 228) tell three mythological stories. In 'Mythologies I' the story is that of the demon Poothana who was sent by king Kamsa, to kill the baby Lord Krishna by feeding poisonous milk. But as the legend goes, the divine child sucked away not only the poisonous milk but her life itself which redeemed her from the curse. In the poem the poet wants 'Terror with a baby face' to suck him dry of this venom and renew his life. 'Mythologies II' has the story of Narasimham as the main image. The demon king Hiranya begets the boon from the gods as :

not to be slain by demon, god, or by
beast, not by day or by night
by no manufactured weapon, not out
of doors nor inside, not in the sky
nor on earth (*CP* : 226)

Therefore, Lord Vishnu takes the incarnation of Narasimham — half lion and half man and kills the demon on the threshold by twilight. The poet now is in a predicament like the demon king and calls upon the divine to 'slay now my faith in doubt,' 'Mythologies III' refers to the Hindu concept of considering sexual union between a lawfully wedded man and woman as the union with the divine :

> She fled his hand as she would a spider,
>
> threw away her modesty, as the rods
> and cones of her eyes gave the world a new bith :
> She saw Him then, unborn, form of forms, the Rider,
>
> His white Bull chewing cud in her backyard.
>
> (*CP* : 228)

The woman who worships Shiva ironically tells her new groom not to touch her, reminding one of the legend of Neelakantar, the Tamil Saivite saint who was told by his wife not to touch her as he had been to other women. However, in the context of the poem, the bride tells her groom not to touch her because she wants to worship Shiva. The poem carries an ironical tone as the statement of Neelakantar's wife is used in a different context and also because the bride finally understands that the lawful union of the body, mind and spirit cannot be anything but divine by the parametres of Hindu religion.

In 'Turning Around' (*CP* : 224) one could very clearly hear voices of the man who has been tethered away from the Indian village to which he once belonged. Cut off from his rural moorings the voice in the poem reminisces the pastures, the sheep and the 'throaty cry' of the shepherd in the village. He nostalgically thinks,

> but what am I to this herd
> of Indian sheep, to be fed
> and sheard or
> slaughtered, or to this man
> who shares a throaty cry
> with his father
> and his father's father
> his cousins and enemies
> for miles around?

one could hear the remorse in the voice that he cannot relate himself to the sheep or to the people who unlike him have still a lineage. He has missed the link with the past of his own land and people, and now turning around he can only be nostalgic.

In the poem titled 'Pain : trying to find a metaphor,' the poet refers to the acid rains and the bonsai tree, both of which are alien to the Indian context. The acid rains about which the scientists are making brainstorms to stop it, happen in the highly industrialised places like the North American cities. Similarly, the bonsai tree is a Japanese art in which trees are made to grow in the stunted form to decorate the interiors.

The fictional speaker in 'In March' (*CP* : 238) dramatising the delerium caused by high fever and third degree burns, picturises the world in his body. The warmth in the blood stream is

> warm as the ocean currents
> that took Aztecs to Mexico.

Fever showed him alegators, Red-hot fish 'white heat of whales,' 'blips and signals of cool silver dolphins,' 'stillness of icebergs' and 'sleepless oceans.' Before the fever he :

> ... ... never knew that [his] Amazon
> flows savage and treacherous
> through [his] Africas...

'No Fifth Man' is based on a Sanskrit parable that illustrates the foolishness of four egoistic brahmins who were well learned. Though they all had the wisdom that is in the shastras, they lacked the practical commonsense. In their blinding ego they hardly realised it and consequent to that, became victims of their own vain knowledge. Like 'Black Hen' this poem is also about writing poetry, which once done takes hold of the creator. The parable is used as a metaphor.

The poem 'Bosnia' is a picture of the atrocities that had been committed in Bosnia, Biafra and Bangladesh during wars. It is the subtle presentation of all the cruelties done to the people of these places which triggers of the sentiments of the readers.

'A Report' lists down the men — Hitler, Stalin, Lenin, Gandhi and King — who created history but are now irrelevant. The ideologies of none of these people which are so varied, are of any use today. They have been totally defeated. Besides their ideologies, values in general itself are in total decay. The after effects of this can be seen in the decay of the cities like Chicago and Zurich where addiction to various things like cocaine and diseases like AIDS which kills a person psychologically and mentally first and then physically, are rampant. The poem takes a quick round, across the globe in reporting the scenes of decay and deterioration.

'The Guru' is poem about the patriarchal, hypocritical gurus who are strewn across the length and breadth of our country. The fictional speaker follows the guru very obediently on all his teachings except on his teaching not to forgive the woman her malice and man his envy because, 'I remembered I was a man born of woman' (251).

'Butcher's Tao' (*CP* : 254) is a poem about the Chinese butchers who practise Taoism — the right way of doing a job, in humility and in piety. The butcher in China is detached and is concentrated only on the job he is doing. He has no personal sentiments towards the animal and hence makes a through profession of the job he has undertaken. He studies the animal thoroughly before slaughtering it, as to how it should be killed so that every part of it could be used. In the process the poet throws light on some of the Chinese customs and rituals as well :

> and the bull
> is now sirloin,
> tenderloin, prime ribs,
> dogbone, two horns,
> for weddings or combs,
> sandals for the pedestrian
> peasant, saddle and rein
> for horse, thong and head
> for kettledrums to scare away
> eclipses from the sun,
> ghosts from processions,
> or summon cities
> to banquets, friends and
> enemies to battle,
> the blood in the bucket
> ready for sprinkling

on children with polio
and village borders.

The poet traces the route of a Vat from Trivandrum to Jerusalem in 'A Copper Vat.' The old copper vat which is about three centuries old was picked 'by a Portuguese galleon from/ a bath house/in Trivandrum.' It was kept in a Boston museum for a brief period and from Boston it is being carried away in a Jerusalem bus. The poem, as is evident, is about on old Indian vat which is an antique and is so artistic, and is plundered out of the country for its artistic value by the European colonisers and kept by the Americans who are crazy about the oriental and taken away to Jerusalem for a price.

In the group of poems titled 'Images' there are about five short poems that are closer to the theme of discussion. The first poem 'Taste' is about the Indian practice of smearing bitter neem paste on the nipples of the mother to wean greedy babies. The poem uses this practice as a metaphor to tell how tastes are cultivated. If 'Spring' makes an image of the Chicago traffic and 'Invisible Bodies' speak of the bodies that lie buried in the streets among the 'gamboge maples,' 'Farewell' portrays the anxiety of the Indian mother when her children fly to America :

... ... you should
not forget your oil bath
every tuesday
when you go to America. (*CP* : 259)

The last poem in the group speaks about the significance of zero and hops from one religous belief to another.

The Mayans had a glyph for zero
he said
the Hindus thought zero was holy
he said
The Jewish god was one, the Buddhist was zero
he said. (*CP* : 263)

This poem exhibits Ramanujan's acquaintance with various philosophies. However, he ends the poem noting that these abstract ideas have no value unless they become real — like the zero having no value unit it follows a real number.

The last poem in the collection taken for study is 'Fear No Fall.' And it tells the legend of the Tamil saint Arunagiri. The saint who squandered his youth is berefet of friends in old age and is steeped in desolation. On repentence, by a divine boon, he becomes a saint, and composes some of the finest lyrics in Tamil in the name of Lord Murugan, who bestows the boon.

A reading of Ramanujan's poems, especially the ones in *The Black Hen*, makes one agree with Desai's observation on his poems in general : At the end of a decade of critical dialogue on Ramanujan's poetry, the opinion that is getting crystallised is that Ramanujan is a significant poet poised between two worlds. The two worlds between which he is poised obviously are the world in which he is born and the one which he knows — which encompasses the natural world and the outer space as well. It then becomes very obvious that the perception of Ramanujan "is not just that of the Hindu or merely an Indian in the sense that he sees only those. His perceptive eye roves wider and the limit of his perception is encompassing a wider area" (Desai : 110). The Indian is indeed predominant but definitely not confrontationary to the hegemonic colonial culture and thereby do not try to revert back to the traditional, the Indian, in a counter hegemonic manner. Instead as mentioned above, his perception is pluralistic accommodating other cultures. This of course, does not point towards assimilation or integration of the others into the Indian or the Indian into the global. Instead, the Indian as well as the others have their own individual borders, and hence make a pattern in the global cultural mosaic. He talks about cultures as old as the Yukon valley culture (which is ten thousand years old) and the recent trends. Through time and space, Ramanujan extends to the borders of the globe out into the outer space and oceans and the natural world. To make it short, Ramanujan proves that "the idea of a pure essential culture is a mythic imposition on the contemporary reality of all societies (Griffith : 437). Ramanujan's perception of the world has the elasticity that simultaneously localises the globe and globalises the local, thwarting the corrosive hegemonising force which may be a threat to the integrity of all peculiarities.

WORKS CITED

Desai, S.K. 1984. "Mixing Memory and Desire : Small-Scale Reflections on the Poetry of A.K. Ramanujan" in M.K. Naik (ed.) *Perspectives on Indian Poetry in English*. New Delhi : Abhinav : 109-123.

Griffith, Gareth. 1992. "Culture and Identity : Politics and Writing in Some Recent Post-Colonial Texts," in Anna Rutherford (ed.) *Commonwealth to Post-Colonial.* Sydney : Dangaroo Press : 430-43.

Rabinow, Paul. 1995. *Symbolic Domination : Cultural Form and Historical Change in Morocoo.* Chicago : University of Chicago Press.

Ramanujan, A.K. 1995. *The Collected Poems of A.K. Ramanujan* (ed.) Vinay Dharwadker. New Delhi : Oxford University Press. Referred to as *CP* in the text.

13

Religious Poetry and Literary Criticism : A Note on A.K. Ramanujan's *Speaking of Siva*

—*RAMA NAIR*

The dialectic of religious narratives has taken on multifaceted dimensions of interpretation in the course of the development of literary history. Religious poetry provides a central framework of reference when one analyses the concept of religion in India. In India, *bhakti* poetry became one of the chief agents of social fusion in the Middle Ages. The *Bhagavata* exalts *bhakti* to mean service to God motivated by an intense love based on unconditional devotion and faith. It is the subject, more than the object of worship that is emphasised in this form of literature. *Sraddha* or faith, as opposed to pure intellectual knowledge is the cornerstone of *bhakti*. In the *Bhagavata*, service to the Lord and surrender to him out of selfless and transcendent love is *bhakti*. *Bhakti* is the intensity of divine love whereby the devotee merges in the Lord. The attitudes of reverence, love, submission, separation and fulfilment are expressed spontaneously by these mystic poets in their lyrics. Mysticism is defined as a belief in or experience of a reality surpassing normal human understanding or experience of a reality, especially a reality perceived as essential to the nature of life (Hanks *et al* : 974). It is a system of contemplative prayer and spirituality aimed at achieving direct intuitive perception of the divine.

Ramanujan's translations of *bhakti* poetry reiterate that the only route to salvation is total surrender to God. This concept seems to have influenced him tremendously in his later years. A collection of his selected poems entitled *The Black Hen* was published posthumously in 1995. The earliest of the poems in this last volume appear to have been written in 1989, in Michigan, and the latest in March or April, 1993. In his first three volumes of poetry written over a span of twenty years, Ramanujan sought to universalise his personal predicament. The main experience in these poems is connected with his family, and a host of relations he left behind in India. In his search for roots, he drifted alone, as the title of his first volume *The Striders* suggests. These poems were chiefly related to the orthodox setting of his brahmin ancestry in South India. It is interesting to observe that in *The Black Hen* written between 1989 and 1993, the poems go beyond the regressive quality of a static tradition. The present, in the wake of Westernization, loosely equated with modernization, is only an amalgam of disintegration. Disintegration involves the breakup of a culture resulting in instability. Without the strong foundation of culture and tradition, the life of the thinly disguised persona in these poems is as sterile as the life around him. In these later poems, Ramanujan chose certain voices, images, and metaphors to articulate his concept of nature and culture. Ultimately, it is the strength and validity of spiritual wisdom over mere scientific knowledge that can lead to the realization of an integrated spiritual self.

One's natural desire for conceptual knowledge has to be renounced in favour of a non-conceptual knowledge that could lead to a whole new mode of knowing and loving in this spiritual wasteland. To Ramanujan, it perhaps lay in an unconditional surrender to God. *The Black Hen*, though it is a testimony to the disintegrating values of our times, also offers a redemptive vision. Appropriately enough, the last poem in this volume is called '*Fear No Fall.*' It tells the story of Arunagiri, '*a truant extraordinary,/escape artist, burglar of hearts*,' '*...unlettered and worthless*' who '*hated temple bells and hypocrisies*' (*CP* : 273). In a vision he is told to sing of '*Murugan*' by an '*Old Man*' who gave him his first line of verse. The spiritual transformation of the wayward Arunagiri into a saint was expressed in his devotional songs that ensnared passers by '*unlocking cages/even* *for mynahs and parrots.*' The poet's spiritual dilemma appears to dissolve as he feels that he too may be redeemed by a Voice which averts his fear of '*falling in the gutters below*' by calling out to him both within and without, 'Fall, fall,/you'll never fear a fall again./fall now!' (*CP* : 275). In *The Black Hen*, poetry when combined with ethical sensibility opens a whole new dimension of positive interpretation by releasing a pluri-dimensionality of meaning. This idea was reinforced by his translations of *bhakti* poetry. In his choice of the works he chose to translate, it is remarkable that a poet so steeped in satire and apparent cynicism, should deliberately and with commitment translate two important volumes of devotional poetry, one in honour of Siva, called '*Speaking of Siva,*' and the other in praise of Visnu called '*Hymns for the Drowning.*'

Ramanujan states in his "Translator's Note," 'A translation has to be true to the translator no less than the original. He cannot jump off his shadow. Translation is a choice, interpretation, an assertion of taste, a betrayal of what answers one's needs......' (Ramanujan 1973 : 12-13). This statement acquires tremendous significance in the light of his own original poetic creativity. A poet expresses himself when he is deeply affected by certain perceptions. A translator chooses certain works to be translated deliberately. It could be because he finds a deep affinity for the work he is translating. His work does not stop at a mere rendering of the linguistic and textual structure of the poem. The repossessing entails a capturing of the essence or soul of the translated work.

'*Speaking of Siva*' was first published in 1973 with a reprint appearing in 1979. It is a book of *Vacanas* or religious lyrics in Kannada free verse. *Vacana* literally means '*saying, thing said.*' The *Vacanas* were written between the tenth and the twelfth century in India by the Virasaiva saints. These saints speak of Siva and speak to Siva. In '*Speaking of Siva,*' A.K. Ramanujan translated into English some of the *Vacanas* of the four great mystic poets of the period — Basavanna, Devara Dasimayya, Mahadeviyakka and Allama Prabhu. The *Vacanas* are *bhakti* poems addressed primarily to Lord Siva. These mystic poets rejected the formal structure of classical Hindu texts. Their *Vacanas* were a revolt against what may be termed as the great tradition of the Vedas — Vedic ritual, caste hierarchy, and pan-Indian deities; and the Little Traditions of the local Puranas — local sacrificial rites, sects, cults, and religious deities. The spontaneity of worship that is characteristic of the *bhakti* movement transcended the barriers of social hierarchies and even religious differences, creating an emotional integration among the people. To the *bhakti* poet, true religion was the religion of the soul, unencumbered by dogmas and rituals. The *bhakti* poet was a visionary and a seer, a mystic of a high order. He was one who revealed his own self-realization so that others could transcend the limits of their finite self to attain a state of spiritual bliss. To the *Vacanakaras* all 'true experience of God is Krpa, grace that cannot be called, recalled, or commanded" (Ramanujan 1973 : 31). The *Vacanas* distinguished between *anubhava*, '*experience*,' and '*anubhāva*,' 'the Experience.' '*Anubhāva*,' the latter, is a search for the 'unmediated vision,' 'the unconditioned act, the unpredictable experience' (Ramanujan, 1973 : 31). The emphasis was on '*the Experience*,' a return to the primordial essence of Being itself, untramelled by prayer, ritual, and sacrificial offerings. As Ramanujan observes, "living in history, time and cliché, one lives in a world of the pre-established, through the received (sruti), and the remembered (smrti). But the experience when it comes comes like a storm to all such husks and labels" (Ramanujan 1973 : 31). The Virasaiva saints rejected both *sruti* and *smriti*. They were concerned with the experience of the now. So their compositions were *Vacanas*, or '*what is said.*' It was concerned with not what was remembered or received, but what was experienced now.

Religious narratives abound with the concept of epiphany, or the moment of transcendence, when the human self merges with the Divine Self in a mystic moment of inexplicable bliss. Writers have always been fascinated with the supernatural or the miraculous. The interpretation of Mephistopheles in Dr. *Faustus*, the witches in *Macbeth*, the ghost in *Hamlet*, the evil spirits and Satan in *Paradise Lost*, will depend to a large extent on one's attitude to mystical experience. Is Mephistopheles a really transcendently existing evil, or a projection of Faustus's own mind? Are the witches in *Macbeth*, the ghost in *Hamlet*, and the evil spirits in *Paradise Lost* real entities, or mere projections of human fear, anger, and hatred that corrode the heart of man? Mysticism leads to greater insight, perception, intuitive power, and even extrasensory perception. But if these attributes are sought for themselves, then they loses their capacity to generate wisdom. But the mystical experiences of saints, which can be used only to engender serenity and beauty, can be used to redefine one's attitude to the miraculous. In romantic literature, the use of the supernatural was considered to be one aspect of the creative imagination. But in *bhakti* poetry, or the poetry of the mystics, mysticism is no longer a metaphor. It is a felt experience. This interior subliminal movement has the capacity to guide one's life, and its major characteristic is that it is motivated by love.

In this paper I have endeavoured to state that when mystical experience becomes a felt experience as in *bhakti* poetry, then the parameters of literary criticism need to be expanded and redefined in terms of the religious experiences. Here the self experiences a foretaste of immortality. It transcends the mere level of intellectual or cognitive perception. So felt experience and creative expression need to be fused, thereby redefining the concept of intellectual cognition and perception in literary criticism.

I have chosen the mystic poet, Mahadeviyakka, to illustrate some of these points. Mahadevi belonged to the twelfth century, and was a contemporary of Basavanna. She was initiated into Siva worship at the age of ten. Legend has it that she fell in love with the form of Siva as Mallikarjuna, translated either as '*Arjuna, Lord of goddess Mallika*,' or as '*the Lord white as Jasmine*.' Most of her *Vacanas* end with the refrain '*O lord white as Jasmine*.' Such a signature, as Ramanujan states, again centers the poem in a locale and a person, relating god to poet, poet to poem, and poem to audience (Ramanujan, 1981 : 163). Like Mira Bai she was married in spirit to her divine lord. But worldly pressures led her to marry Kausika, or the chieftain of the land. However, she scorned all earthly obligations and affiliations, and set out '*wild and god intoxicated*' in search of her Lord. Her *Vacanas* record this search which follow all the phases of human love as exemplified in Sanskrit poetry. The three aspects of this love are '*love forbidden, love in separation and love in union*' (Ramanujan, 1973 : 11). The different phases of human love are the different stages of mystic ascent. In her quest for ecstasy she defies society and her role as a woman. She died into '*Oneness with Siva*' when she was barely in her twenties. The conflict that is apparent in a forbidden love is expressed thus,

Husband inside,
Lover outside.
I can't manage them both. (Ramanujan, 1973 : 127)

The pain of separation is evident in these lines

Not seeing you
in the hill, in the forest
from tree to tree
I roamed,
    Searching, gasping;
    Lord, my lord, come
    show me your kindness. (Ramanujan, 1973 : 119)

The ecstasy of love in union is illustrated in the following lines :

Locks of shining red hair
a crown of diamonds
small beautiful teeth
and eyes in a laughing face
that light up fourteen world—
    I saw his glory
    and seeing, I quell today
    the famine in my eyes. (Ramanujan, 1973 : 120)

In *Vacana* poetry, the devotee moves from the outer world to the inner. All experiences of the outside world merge into an experience of actually seeing Siva in all things. The devotee's heart is exalted and she begins to see the radiance of the Lord in herself. Mahadevi in *Vacana* no : 50 questions "when I didn't know myself/where were you?/Like the colour in the gold,/you were in me./I saw in you,/lord white as jasmine,/the paradox of your being/in me/without showing a limb' (Ramanujan,

1973 : 119). In the next stage, the devotee is with the Lord, and 'suffers only as a living woman suffers her lover's absence, living in two worlds, half-mad, half in coma.' Many of Mahadevi's *Vacanas* belong to this phase. She cries 'Four parts of the day/I grieve for you./Four parts of the night/I'm mad for you.' And finally, "O fathers/why do you bother/with this woman? /She has no strength of limb,/has lost the world,/lost power of will, turned devotee,/she has lain down/ with the Lord, white as jasmine,/and has lost caste.' In the last stage there is no worship anymore 'for who is out there to receive such worship? This is Oneness or aikyasthala. Like space joining space, water water, the devotee dissolves nameless in the Lord, who is not another' (Ramanujan, 1973 : 174).

In the Hebrew-Christian tradition it is affirmed that the highest ecstasies are only a token of the final experience of God. They are never the last stage. Consciousness of the absolute is never direct. The most sublime states of consciousness are only a beginning, because there is always something beyond. In this tradition, the final cosmic union with Christ is possible only through death, and resurrection. But *bhakti* poetry involves a fullness of being in which the dualistic concept of Nara-narayana, or I and Thou, blend into the one of holistic consciousness. The ontic merges with the ontological, and creates a sense of divine rapture and aesthetic pleasure. If mystical rapture is taken as a fundamental step towards self-realisation, then all religious narratives lead to a redefinition of the self. If this is the case, then the experience of the supernatural or the miraculous need not be considered as mental aberrations, or hallucinations of a diseased imagination. In the *Vacanas*, felt experience and creative expression fuse to engender a form of literature that is at once credible and enlightening. In effect, it would imply that reason can be transcended here leading to a redefinition of literary cognition and perception. Literary criticism should therefore include a level of critical perception that encompasses the motif of religious experiences as an acceptable norm of literary appreciation.

As an expatriate, Ramanujan's overwhelming concern with his Indian past speaks of an intellect and a soul that was inextricably bound and sustained by a tradition that was enriching and fulfilling. '*Speaking of Siva*,' Ramanujan's translations of the Kannada *Vacanas*, is perhaps the solution to many of the gripping dilemmas of the modern man.

WORKS CITED

Hanks, Patrick *et al* (eds.). 1984. *Collins Dictionary of the English Language*. London : Collins.

Ramanujan A.K. 1995. *The Collected Poems of A.K. Ramanujan* (ed.) Vinay Dharwadker. New Delhi : Oxford Univ. Press, Referred to as *CP* in the text.

——, (Tr.) 1981. *Hymns for the Drowning*. Princeton : Univ. of Princeton Press.

——, (Tr) 1973. *Speaking of Siva*. Harmondsworth : Penguin.

14

Network of Relations : Cross-Fertilization in Ramanujan's Translations and Poetry

—RITA KOTHARI

In an insightful article on Ramanujan, Vinay Dharwadker, refers to him as a "postcolonial cosmopolitan" who used whatever was at hand and changed it, "ever so slightly" so that connections between past and present, ancient and modern sensibilities and East and West continue to be formed rather than broken (Dharwadker : 91-97). Unlike the currently strident spokespersons of the third world, Ramanujan's artistic conception has helped him in 'connecting' and 'joining' cultures rather than dividing them. In his essay Dharwadker points at the 'outcome' of Ramanujan's forays into different temporal and cultural spaces. What interests me however are the processes by which connections are formed. In simple terms, I wish to show how Ramanujan's journeying in various disciplines; his inwardness with Kannada and Tamil cultures, his insights into the West and what it represented — crisscrossed with each other, building (to use Dharwadker's phrase) a 'network of relations.' Hence an assessment of individual parts in Ramanujan's literary output is a falsification of the wholeness and continuity characterising his entire *ouvré*. Ramanujan's views on cultures, families, relationships, selfhood, form the basis of a world-view that was the shaping principle behind a lot of his work. As it is beyond the scope of this paper to study this principle in relation to Ramanujan's entire literary output, I shall restrict myself to it by examining two very significant and concurrent activities in Ramanujan's life — his poetry and his translations.

The paper is structured in three sections. The first section is an overview of the context of the sixties which produced Ramanujan as a poet and a translator. Section II delineates preoccupations, themes and techniques that recur in his poetry and the relation of these with his translations — links that manifest themselves through various tangible and intangible forms. Section III comments upon the obfuscation of 'primary' and 'secondary' activities that emerges out of tracing the cultural and literary 'origins' of Ramanujan's work.

I

Before embarking upon internal connections between various literary activities, it is important to delineate contexts that underlie Ramanujan's emergence as a poet and translator. When Ramanujan started writing in the sixties, Indian English poetry had taken a very significant turn in form and content. Among developments that took place from *within* the body of Indian English poetry a principal one was the break from the Aurobindian phase of romantic/lyrical poetry of the pre-independence era. Romantic and Victorian verse was giving way to a terse, ironic idiom in the work of Modernist poets in England and America and Indian poets writing in English as well as other languages followed the new change. In a historic manner, P. Lal's early publications from his Writers Workshop announced the irrelevance of pre-Independence poetry and established a new credo for poetry in postcolonial India. The workshop served as an ideological and material forum for all those who wanted to express themselves in English and in a specific way. Out of this combination of English language and modernist affiliations emerged, among many good and bad poets, distinguished poets such as Nissim Ezekiel, A.K. Ramanujan and Arun Kolatkar. It needs to be stated here that Ramanujan was also a product of Kannada literature and consequently affected by developments that took place within that literary-linguistic arena. He had begun to write when the fiery Gopalkrishna Adiga had newly burst in on the Kannada literary scene, leading to what came to be called the Navya School. The Navya School fought against the romantic solipsism that ignored the ills of the actual world. By no stretch of imagination may Ramanujan be considered a Socialist, but the movement away from the Romantic phase in Kannada must have also been one of the factors determining Ramanujan's idiom in the years to come.

Coming back to the literary scene in fifties, we must bear in mind that the Writers Workshop was one of the very few, and for some time the only, publishing house available to Indians writing in English. In the absence of a stable pro-English policy in post-Independence India, the situation of the English language was too precarious for publishing to be considered as a viable commercial activity. (The sixties is a crucial period in that regard, English was officially entrenched in India.) The Workshop also served as a forum for translation (or in P. Lal's case, 'transcreation') activity. In fact, some of Ramanujan's contemporaries had parallel careers in English and regional contexts. For instance, Arun Kolatkar and Dilip Chitre translated from Marathi, Arvind Krishna Mehrotra from Hindi, Jayanta Mahapatra from Oriya and R. Parthasarathy from Tamil into English. Since the language of the new Modernist (influenced by Anglo-American Modernism) poetry in English written by Indian poets was unsentimental and terse, this idiom was for the first time made available for translation also. Looking at the phenomenon of writing and translating in English from the sixties onwards, it has been noted that such developments were expressive and constitutive of a "complex continuum between English and the various Indo-Aryan and Dravidian languages" (Aparna *et al* :). This was also in tandem with Indian English criticism which was acquiring specific local concerns and cultural immediacy. In fact writing in and translating into English continued in a simultaneous fashion and searched for paradigms to fit both exercises in juxtaposition. However, of all the poets who began parallel careers in both activities, it was only in Ramanujan that both roles merged and collapsed.

II

The section that follows is an attempt to show linkages and similarities in Ramanujan's poetry and translations. Needless to say that this kind of exercise of pointing similarities is not fully categorical, since one-to-one correspondences are neither possible nor desirable to establish. Sometimes continuities manifest themselves in specific word choice, phrases and verbal or non-verbal techniques, and at times only through shades and hints of meanings. As far as Ramanujan is concerned, a range of devices such as ironic understatement, wit, word play and economy of expression cut across his translations as well as his poetry. For instance, both "Pain : trying to find a metaphor" and "Death in Search of a Comfortable Metaphor" written in 1992 echo the following vacana from the *Speaking of Siva* :

> I went out :
> It was like the sudden dawn
> Of a million million suns
> A ganglion of lightnings
> For my wonder
> O Lord of caves
> If you are light
> There can be no metaphor.

Here is Ramanujan's English poem :

> Grandmother's version
> of how scorpions die
> to give birth
> may not be true
> but sounds right....
>
> But when did elephants
> console the living
> left behind by a death?

("Death in Search of a Comfortable Metaphor," *CP* : 273)

The spiritual commitment of the vacanakara is profoundly and economically communicated in the first example from the *Speaking of Siva*. While it is undeniable that the content of English translation is from the original Kannada, some tone and texture of the speaking voice, the imagistic complexity of pithy phrases that also appears as 'simplicity' of medieval poetry is neither clearly 'original' nor 'translation.' The same quality is inherent in the second instance from Ramanujan's English poem where the experience of death is communicated in a half-serious, euphemistic manner in order to understate the horror or make it appear an everyday conversation. In another case, there are similar shades in terms of words and context. The ironic anti-climax of the nameless and non-descript "identical twins" in the poem "A River" written in English is like the anonymous "daughter of the hill tribe" in the translation "Murukan's Places." This is conveyed in both poems through insignificant markers of differentiation and identity so that the object of worship (river in one case and Murukan in the other) gains importance.

> where the daughter of the hill tribe
> worships...
> wearing two cloths
> different in colour and kind
>
> (Murukan : His Places)
>
> ....
> and one pregnant woman
> expecting identical twins
> with no moles on their bodies,
> with different-coloured diapers
> to tell them apart. (A River, *CP* : 39)

Ramanujan's poems in English "As Eichmann Said, My Brother Said" and poems like "Love 1 : what she said" or "Love 2 : what he said, remembering" replicate the oral tale-like pattern of the akam poems. There is similarity of structure such that the original English poem reads like the modern recreation of an ancient poem resulting in a disorienting sense of what is new and what is old. Here is an excerpt from "As Eichmann Said, My Brother Said" followed by a classical Tamil poem translated by Ramanujan :

> As Eichmann said, the trains
> ran like a dream, my brother said
> in the city square and the stocks
> were harrumphing bulls on TV....
>
> As Eichmann said, how can I
> talk about it now
> after all these years
> of not remembering and not

forgetting either? That was
then, now is now, my brother said.

What She Said

the bare root of the bean is pink
like the leg of a jungle hen,
and herds of deer attack its overripe pods.
for the harshness
of this season of morning dew
there is no cure

but the breast of my man.

Bruce King notes that "the complexity, instability and irony of Ramanujan's poems seem very modern, as is the way they appear to offer themselves as imagistic statements to be appreciated and interpreted as the reader wishes. But acquaintance with various introductions, prefaces and afterwords to Ramanujan's translations of medieval Kannada and Tamil verse reveals that what seems original and modern is partly based on older poetic conventions" (King : 116). King's remark implies that Ramanujan's poetry did not impose modernist features upon his translations but rather that from his experience of translation Ramanujan was bringing older poetic conventions and these coincided with modernist trends in poetry. This throws up very interesting questions about the enterprise of modernity and modernism, originality and translation, but we shall come to that later.

Once again I want to turn to Ramanujan's poetry, and especially his collection *Relations*. The tenor of this collection — the complex nature of family and relations is aptly indicated in the epigraph. The epigraph is from Ramanujan's translation of a classical Tamil poem in the akam genre :

Like a hunted deer
on the wide white
salt land,

    a flayed hide
    turned inside out,

one may run,
escape.

But living
among relations
binds the feet. (*CP* : 56)

The epigraph defines and communicates the poet's ambivalent attitude towards the family which now creates, now binds, building a domestic sphere from which there is no escape. The impurity of the 'self' that is never itself, but everything else around it is clearly a product of these binding relations and therefore the "Self-Portrait" :

I resemble everyone
but myself, and sometimes see
in shop-windows,
despite the well-known laws
of optics,
the portrait of a stranger,
date unknown,
often unsigned in a corner
by my father. (*CP* : 23)

The legacy from father to son to son is further explored in "Extended Family" in *Second Sight* (1986). The self is created by and subsumed into the flux of a joint family. In fact the notion of 'self' as the core with concentric circles of family and society is integral to Ramanujan's poetry. It is not dissimilar to the arrangement of akam (interior) and puram (exterior) spaces that lock in their embrace a vulnerable and susceptible self.

King notes that "the understated, neutral standing at a distance from description can be found in the Tamil classics he translated. The use of the self as a centre for a poem filled with ironies, which unpredictably changes direction and attitudes and which resist conclusion, is within the tradition of medieval saints' poetry" (King : 116). There is no doubt that then Ramanujan's poetry was encompassing in its fold diverse experiential realities and techniques encountered in his translations. At the same time, this is not simply one kind of craft affecting another. As a poet and as a translator Ramanujan was also affected by his reading of Yeats, Eliot and other moderns writers. Ramanujan acknowledged the role English literary masters played in his translation activity, when he once said, "If I didn't know Pound or Donne or Shakespeare's sonnets I would not have picked up the pieces I did" (Daruwalla : 18). The question is not what affected what, but where did it all begin? The question is one of origins, hence very difficult to answer. However, some of the implications surrounding the question are discussed in the next section.

III

In the previous section we noticed how Ramanujan admitted the impact of English poets on the choices for translation. He even said "The metaphysical poets were very important to me. Ezra Pound was very important to my Tamil Poetry. He made me look at Tamil Poetry differently" (Ibidem). The process of reclaiming poets of the past was facilitated by the internalization of modern European poets. In this situation the postcolonial poet-translator is not engaged in a 'pure' enterprise of translating medieval and classical poets. The reading, interpretation and the translation of ancient poets into English is coloured by English poets. The ancient and the modern, the Indian and the Western have criss-crossed in the very act of translation. This implies translation not at a linguistic level alone, but also at a cultural level. It reinforces the view of translation as seeking to articulate hybrid intercultural spaces and identities. At the same time, Ramanujan's modernism is not a purely European brand of Modernism, it has been affected by the succinct and epigrammatic quality of the virsaiva poets and also of the classical Tamil poets. The postcolonial poet here is accessing cultures distant in time and space and the poetry emerging out of such simultaneity is continuous with both past and present. In a cycle of hybrid literary influences and sensibilities, how do you trace the 'origins?' The transference of cultural meanings from modernist to medieval, and all of that to contemporary is a story of circular narratives.

The plural nature of literary influences underlying Ramanujan's work problematizes the notion of 'translation' as 'what comes after the original.' His translations have not merely 'contributed' to his poetry, but functioned as an inseparable part of its linguistic and cultural life. This broadens the meaning of translation and is consistent with a postcolonial concept of translation as metaphor. A step further in the same argument, is the stand that the broadening of 'translation' also leads to a broadening of the 'original.' When meanings and forms of the 'primary' and the 'secondary' activity, from past to present and the East and the West fluidly flow into each other, the notion of 'originality' requires redefinition. It does not then consist in what is new, but in an intricate and subtle connection of the old and the new. In the Afterword to *Poems of Love and War*, Ramanujan himself asserts that "the notion of originality is itself a recent convention" and it implies a misleading disjunction of traditions and individual talent (Ramanujan : 1985).

The disjunction of tradition and modernity or past and present is never complete enough to mark out the new from the old. Traditions are never dead nor fixed and each re-newal modifies the tradition. In the postcolonial scenario, every 'original' act involves translation. Rushdie refers to his tribe as "translated men" (Rushdie : 17). In the final analysis then, this paper has sought to highlight this sense of continuity in Ramanujan communicated by him so beautifully in his acknowledgements, 'What do I have that I have not received?' (Ramanujan : 1973).

WORKS CITED

Aparna and Vinay Dharwadkev. 1998. "Indian English Literature : Literary and Commercial Success" in V.N. Narayanan and Jyoti Sabharwal (eds.) *India at 50 : Bliss of Hope and Burden of Reality*. New Delhi : Sterling.

Daruwalla, Keki N. 1994. "Ramanujan : The Expatriate Local," *Indian Literature* 162 : 17-25.

Dharwadker, Vinay. 1994. "Postcolonial Cosmopolitanism : A Note on A.K. Ramanujan's Theory and Practice of Criticism and Translation." *Indian Literature*, 160 : 91-97.

King, Bruce. 1987. *Modern Indian Poetry in English*. New Delhi : Oxford University Press.

Ramanujan, A.K. 1995. *The Collected Poems of A.K. Ramanujan* (ed.) Vinay Dharwadker. New Delhi : Oxford University Press. Referred to as *CP* in the text.

———, 1985. *Poems of Love and War*. New Delhi : Oxford University Press.

———, 1973. *Speaking of Siva*. Harmondsworth : Penguin.

Rushdie, Salman. 1991. *Imaginary Homelands*. London : Granta Books.

APPENDIX-A

Bruce King's Letter

411 South College Avenue, Muncie, Indiana 47303, USA
Telephone : 317-282-3569
Fax : 317-285-8980, c/o Adele King
E-mail : 00ACKING@BSUVAX1

Dear Dr. Pandey,

I can not promise you an essay on Raman, although I would very much like to write one. I am very much behind with contracted work and when I do manage that I have other contracted work to begin on. You probably do not know that when I returned to the USA after many years of professorships abroad, I could not get a regular university position here. Affirmative Action policies meant that there was no more hiring of senior white males, and it was assumed that any "minority" person must know more about postcolonial literatures than a white American. By a curious reverse discrimination skin colour counts for more than publications or actual research. This means that I must spend much time either as a visiting professor outside of the USA or preparing grant applications; both of which take time which ideally should be spent on research and writing. It also means that I now usually write for money, although I still make exceptions for worthy reasons.

By the time this letter reaches you I will probably be teaching in Taiwan for the year. So there is no point in my promising you anything. But keep me informed how your issue is progressing and if, as sometimes happens, the muse descends and offers me something worthwhile on Raman I will send it to you. (Keep using my American address.) I came to know him rather well and might write about him as a person rather than a poet or scholar.

Some people who might ask [sic] to contribute are Arvind K. Mehrotra (at the U of Allahabad), Gieve Patel (who lives in Bombay), R. Parthasarathy (who now teaches in the English Dept., Skidmore College, New York), Nissim Ezekiel (who you can still reach through P.E.N., Bombay), Adil Jussawalla, Vinay Dharwadker (English Dept., University of Oklahoma, Norman, OK.) and Edward C. Dimock, Jr. (Prof. of South Asian Languages and Civilizations at the University of Chicago), David Grene (U. of Chicago) and Wendy Doniger (also U of Chicago South Asian Languages), Rukun Advani (Oxford U P, Delhi). They knew him well and could write on aspects of his life and work. They could also suggest others. His former wife Molly Daniels has his manuscripts including new unpublished poems. You could write to her c/o Dimock or the South Asian Languages Dept. When you write to any of the above you can mention my name except in the case of Grene and Doniger who I don't know. I have never spoken with Molly Daniels but I am told that she knows of my existence. Raman used to spend time in Bangalore studying folklore, but I don't know who you should contact there. You might also try U.R. Anantha Murthy (now Vice Chancellor of some university in Kerala I believe). There are a couple of other names that I don't remember at present. One was the head editor at O.U.P. before Advani. He now has his own publishing house. Dayal or something like that. You could ask Arvind, Adil, Nissim, etc., for the name and address.

Sorry not to send you the addresses, but I really can not spare the time to look them up. You can probably get most of them through Oxford U.P., in New Delhi.

You might try to find critics who could write about his poetry in Kannada and Tamil, his translations, his study of Indian folklore, his study of and use of linguistics, his early Mysore days (and the Kannada modern poetry scene at that time), his interest in psychiatry, his use of Sanskrit classical literature (which I think he mostly knew in translation, although he was teaching himself Sanskrit), his relationship to modern European literature, the Buddhist influence on his thought, may be something about his father, his relationship to south Indian Brahmanism, his poetics or theory of art, his relationship to India, his verse forms, the relationship of his poetry to Indian poetic traditions, his fusion of Indian and European thought, his Chicago poems.

Some of his early poems are in the early issues of *Quest*. They have never been republished. They show that early on he had a curious relationship to Brahmanism and Indian spirituality. Like a Catholic theologian quarreling with his church. Maybe you could find them and ask Molly to republish them. She should also have the translations of his Kannada poem she was working on for the past few years. P. Lal keeps everything and may have some early letters or poems.

If you are going to do this issue then do it well. Maybe spend a day or so with Arvind Mehrotra in Allahabad and discuss it with him and who should write for it. They knew each other well, respected each other's work and discussed their plans with each other. Take your time. Raman was major poet and scholar by international standards, but his poetry did not get the attention it deserved because no one had the same range of reading and culture he had. This is a chance to publish some serious commentary on Raman and set critics in the right directions. But it will take time and much work writing to people.

Yours sincerely,

Bruce King

[This undated letter was received sometime in the last week of August 1993.]

APPENDIX-B

Keki N. Daruwalla's Letter

K.N. Daruwalla

79, Mount Kailash,
SFS Apts, Pocket-A,
New Delhi - 110 065
Tel. : 6441574
November 17, 1999

Dear Dr. Pandey,

I was abroad from 16th October to 8th November and returned to find your letter. I am sorry I missed you in Delhi. It would have been so nice to meet up with you and have a long chat.

As regards the meaningful information about A.K. Ramanujan, I looked up my records — though not the essay you mentioned. When I met AKR at the IIC, there was no paper with me and I made my notes on a paper napkin which I still preserve. My notes indicate that he had mentioned that his poems 'Anxiety' and 'Conventions of Despair' had been written in 1957, perhaps in Pune. 'A Hindu to his Body' and 'Still Another view of Grace' were published in Quest (1955-56). 'Army Ants,' 'Small Town South India' and 'Eyes, Ears, Noses and a thing about Touch' were written in 1952. This does not preclude the fact that he may have written more poems before he went to USA.

Twenty five of his translations which appear in his book 'Speaking of Shiva' were taken by him to USA when he went there first. I hope these comments answer some of your questions. It is quite possible that he may have had almost a full volume of poems when he went to the USA.

With regards

Yours sincerely,
(K.N. Daruwalla)

Dr. Surya Nath Pandey,
Professor of English,
Banaras Hindu University.
Varanasi - 221005

Annotated Bibliography

PRIMARY SOURCES

1. (a) Poetry

The Striders. 1966. London : Oxford.

Relations. 1971. London : Oxford.

Selected Poems. 1976. London : Oxford.

Second Sight. 1986. New York : Oxford.

The Collected Poems. 1995. New Delhi : Oxford.

[Also includes the unpublished *The Black Hen*.]

(b) Uncollected Poems

(i) 'I Listened,' 'Carpe Diem,' 'The Whip,' 'The Gnomes,' 'In the Past' and 'Two Days' in 1989. *An Anthology of Indian English Poetry*. Hyderabad : Orient Longman : 41-44.

(ii) 'Stranger.' 1990-91. *Poetry Review* : 80 : 4 : 38.

(iii) 'Of Curves.' quoted in 1981. Amanuddin, Syed. *World Poetry in English*. New Delhi : Sterling : 125.

(iv) 'No Dream, No Symbol,' 'The Body as the Translator,' 'Of Corruption,' 'Madura : Two Movements.' 1957-58. *Quest* : 3 : Aug.-Feb.

2. Prose

(a) *The Collected Essays*. 1999. New Delhi : Oxford.

Contains the following essays

"Where Mirrors Are Windows : Towards an Anthology of Reflections" : 6-33. First published in 1989, *History of Religions* : 28 : 3 : 187-216.

[Final version of a Radhakrishnan Memorial Lecture in All Souls' College, Oxford University in May 1988, though first drafted for a Conference paper delivered in Germany in 1985.]

"Is There an Indian Way of Thinking? An Informal Essay" : 34-51. First published in 1989. *Contribution to Indian Sociology* : 23 : 1 : Jan-June : 41-58. Also in 1990 in Marriott, McKim. Ed. *India Through Hindu Categories*. New Delhi : Sage : 41-58 and in 1990. *The Book Review* : 14 : 1 : Jan-Feb : 18-23.

[Privately printed revision (1986) of an informal essay for a "Workshop on the Hindu Person" held at the Univ. of Chicago, 1980.]

"Towards an Anthology of City Images : 52-72. First published in 1970 in Fox, Richard G. Ed. *Urban India : Society, Space and Image*. Durham, NC : Duke University.

"Food for Thought : Towards an Anthology of Hindu Food-Images" : 73-95. First published in 1992 in Khare, R.S. Ed. *The Eternal Food : Gastronomic Ideas and Experiences of Hindus and Buddhists*. Albany : State Univ. of New York Press : 221-50.

[Paper delivered at Symposium on food, Sixth International Conference on Semiotics and Structural Studies, Central Institute of Indian Languages, Mysore, Jan. 1985.]

"Language and Social Change : The Tamil Example" : 96-114. First published in 1968 in Drake, Robert. Ed. *Problems of Modernisation in South India*. Durham NC : Duke University.

"Some Thoughts on 'Non-Western' Classics : With Indian Examples" : 115-23. First published posthumously in 1994. *World Literature Today* : 68 : 2 : 331 : 34.

[Edited version of a lecture-text initially drafted in 1991.]

"Three Hundred *Ramayanas* : Five Examples and Three Thoughts on Translation" : 131-60. First published in 1991 in Richman, Paula Ed. *Many Ramayanas : The Diversity of a Narrative Tradition in South Asia*. Berkeley : Univ. of California Press : 22-49.

[Paper presented at the Conference on Comparative Civilizations, Univ. of Pittsburgh, February 1987.]

"Repetition in the *Mahabharata*" : 161-83. First published in 1991 in Sharma, Arvind. Ed. *Essays on the Mahabharata*. Leiden : Brill : 419-43.

[Extensively reworked version of an original Seminar paper "Towards a Structural Analysis of the *Mahabharata*," held at the Univ. of Chicago, 1968.]

"Classics Lost and Found" : 184-96. First published in 1989 in Borden, C.M. Ed. *Contemporary India : Essays on the Uses of Tradition*. New Delhi : Oxford : 131-46.

"Form in Classical Tamil Poetry" : 197-218. First published in 1971 in Sjoberg, A.F. Ed. *Symposium on Dravidian Civilization*. Austin, Texas : Jenkins Publishing Company : 73-106.

"On Translating a Tamil Poem" : 219-31. First published in 1989 in Warren, Rosanna. Ed. *The Art of Translation : Voices from the Field*. Boston : North-Eastern Univ. Press : 47-63

[Developed version of an early lecture entitled "On Translating an Indian Poem" delivered at New York University in 1968.]

"On Women Saints" : 270-78.

[Corrected copy of the essay published in 1982 in Hawley, John S. and Donna M. Wulf Eds. *The Divine Consort*. Berkeley : Berkeley Religious Studies Series.]

"Men, Women and Saints" : 279-94.

[Lecture delivered at the Centre for World Religions at Harvard University, 1976.]

"The Myths of *Bhakti* : Images of Siva in Saiva Poetry" : 295-308. First published in 1984 in Meister, Michael W. Ed. *Discourses on Siva : Proceedings of a Symposium on the Nature of Religious Imagery*. Philadelphia : University of Pennsylvania Press.

[Enlarged version of a paper for a conference on 'The Manifestations of Siva' held at the University of Pennsylvania in 1981.]

"Why an Allama Poem Is Not a Riddle : An Anthological Essay" : 309-23.

[One of the last pieces of criticism composed before his death in July 1993.]

"Varieties of *Bhakti*" : 324-31. First published in 1967 in *The Yearbook of Comparative Literature.*

"On Bharati and His Prose Poems" : 332-43.

[Written in 1983 it forms Introduction to his unpublished translation of Subramania Bharati's prose poems.]

"The Clay Mother-in-Law : A South Indian Folktale" : 352-57. First published in 1956 in *Southern Folklore Quarterly* : 20 : September.

"Some Folktales from India" : 358-68. First published in 1956 in *Southern Folklore Quarterly* : 19 : June.

"Hanchi : A Kannada Cinderella" : 369-76. First published in 1982 in Dundes, A. Ed. *Cinderella : A Folklore Casebook.* New York : Garland : 259-73.

[Developed version of a lecture entitled "Three Cinderellas" delivered at the Centre for Psychosocial Studies, Chicago in 1981.]

"The Indian Oedipus" : 377-97. First published in 1972 in Poddar, A. Ed. *Indian Literature : Proceedings of a Seminar*. Simla : Indian Institute of Advanced Studies : 127-37. Also in 1983 in Edmunds, Lowell and Dundes Alan. Eds. *Oedipus : A Folklore Casebook.* New York : Garland : 235-61, rptd. 1995. Madison : Univ. of Wisconsin Press : 234-61 and in 1999 in Vaidyanathan T.G. and Jeffrey Kripal Eds. *Vishnu on Freud's Desk : A Reader in Psychoanalysis and Hinduism.* New Delhi : Oxford : 109-36.

[Revised version of a conference paper presented at Indian Institute of advanced Studies, Simla in 1971.]

"The Prince Who Married His Own Left Half" : 398-411. First published in 1986 in Case, Margaret and N. Gerald Barrier Eds. *Aspects of India : Essays in Honour of Edward Cameron Dimock, Jr.* New Delhi : Manohar for American Institute of Indian Studies : 1-15.

"A Flowering Tree : A Woman's Tale" : 412-28.

"Towards a Counter-system : Women's Tales" : 429-47. First published in 1991 in Appadurai, Arjun *et al* Eds. *Gender Genre and Power in South Asian Expressive Traditions*. Philadelphia : Univ. of Pennsylvania Press, 33-55.

"Telling Tales" : 448-62. First published in 1989 *Daedalus* : 118 : 4 : Fall : 239-61 and also in 1991 *Indian Horizons* : 40 : 1-2 : 1-19.

[Developed version of a conference paper entitled 'Tale and Teller in South India' delivered at the Sixth Meeting of the International Association for the Study of Folk-narratives, Edinburgh in 1979.]

"Tell It to the Walls : On Folktales in Indian Culture" : 463-84. First published in 1992 in Gordon, Leonard A. and Philip Oldenburg Eds. *Indian Briefing*. Boulder, Colorado : Westview Press.

"Two Realms of Kannada Folklore" : 485-512. First published in 1986 in Ramanujan A.K. and Stuart H. Balckburn. Eds. *Another Harmony : New Essays on the Folklore of India*. Berkeley : Univ of California Press : 41-75.

"On Folk Mythologies and Folk Puranas" : 513-31. First published in 1993 in Doniger, Wendy. Ed. *Purana Perennis : Reciprocity and Transformation in Hindu and Jaina Texts*. Albany : State Univ. of New York Press : 101-20.

"Who Needs Folklore" : 532-52. First published in 1990 in University of Hawaii's South Asia Occasional Paper Series, Honolulu. Also in 1994 *Indian Literature* : 162 : Jul.-Aug. : 93-106.

[Written as the First Rama Watumull Distinguished Lecture on India and delivered at the University of Hawaii on 3 March 1988.]

(b) Uncollected Essays

"The Structure of Variation : A Study in Caste Dialects" in 1968 in Singer, Milton and Bernard S. Cohen. Eds.

Structure and Change in Indian Society. Chicago : Aldine Press.

Fifteen articles to the 'Encyclopaedia of Oriental Literatures' Section on Dravidian Literatures in the *Encyclopaedia Britannica* (1974).

"Parables and Commonplaces" in 1982 in Amirthanaygam, Guy. Ed. *Writers in East-West Encounter : New Cultural Bearings*. London : Macmillan : 138-49.

"Contemporary Indian Poetry" in 1983. *Financial Express* : 6 Mar. : 5 : 3-8.

"Can You Call Him the 'immersed one'?" in 1983. *Times of India* : 31 Jul. : VI : 3-8.

"Talking to God in the Mother-Tongue" in 1992. *India International Centre Quarterly* : 19 : 4 : Winter : 53-64.

3. Translations into English

Fifteen Poems from a Classical Tamil Anthology. 1965. Calcutta : Writers Workshop.

[Only fourteen poems were printed.]

The Interior Landscape : Love Poems from a Classical Tamil Anthology. 1967. Bloomington : Indiana University Press.

[Contains *Fifteen Poems from a Classical Tamil Authology plus new poems*.]

Selected Poems by G. Sankara Kurup. 1969. Calcutta : Dialogue.

Speaking of Siva. 1973. Harmondsworth : Penguin.

Samskara : A Rite for a Dead Man by U.R. Anantha Murthy. 1976. New Delhi : Oxford.

Hymns for the Drowning : Poems for Visnu by Nammalvar. 1981. Princeton : Princeton Univ. Press.

Poems of Love and War : From the Eight Anthologies and the Ten Long Poems of Classical Tamil. 1985. New York : Columbia Univ. Press.

Folktales from India : A Selection of Oral Tales from Twenty-Two Languages. 1991. New York : Pantheon.

4. Works in Collaboration

Some Kannada Poems (translated with M.G. Krishnamurthy). 1966. Calcutta : Writers Workshop.

The Song of the Earth and Other Poems by M. Gopalkrishna Adiga (Translated with Michael Garman and Rajeev Taranath). 1968. Calcutta : Writers Workshop.

The Literatures of India : An Introduction (edited with Edward C. Dimock, Jr, *et al.*) 1975. Chicago : University of Chicago Press.

Indian Poetry Today (translated modern Malayalam poems with K.M. George). 1980. New Delhi : Indian Council of Cultural Relations.

"From Classicism to *Bhakti*" (with Norman Cutler). Early 1980s. *Essays on Gupta Culture.*

Another Harmony : New Essays on the Folklore of India (edited with Stuart H. Blackburn). 1986. Berkeley : University of California Press.

The Oxford Anthology of Modern Indian Poetry (edited with Vinay Dharwadker). 1994. New Delhi : Oxford University Press.

When God Is a Customer : Telugu Courtesan Songs by Ksetrayya and others (edited with V. Narayan Rao and David Shulman). 1994. California : University of California Press.

5. Works in Kannada

Proverbs. 1955. Dharwar : Karnataka University.

Haladi Meenu (The Yellow Fish) by Molly Ramanujan (Translation). 1966. Dharwar : Manohar Granthamala.

Hokkulalli Huvilla (No Lotus in the Navel). 1969. Dharwar : Manohar Granthamala.

Mattu Itara Padyagalu (And Other Poems). 1977. Dharwar : n.p.

Mattobbana Atmacaritre (Another Man's Autobiography) 1978. Dharwar : Manohar Granthamala.

Kuntobille. 1990. Dharwar : Manohar Granthamala.

'Hopscotch,' 'When Meditation Works' and 'The Upanishad Next Door' (Translations of Kannada poems by B.C. Ramachandra Sharma). 1994. *Indian Literature* : 162 : Jul.-Aug. : 81-83

"Annayya's Anthropology" (Translation of a Kannada story by M.N. Chakravorthy). 1973. *Times Weekly* (Bombay) : 6 May : 13-20. And also by Manu Shetty. 1994. *Indian Literature* : 162 : Jul.-Aug. : 84-92.

6. Works Unpublished/Incomplete

1. "Bharati and His Prose Poems" (1983).
2. A Substantial Selection of Poems by about twenty post-Independence Kannada poets.
3. *A Flowering Tale and Other Oral Tales from the Kannada*. (a large collection of orally narrated stories).
4. Some Eighty-eight poems not included in *The Collected Poems*.
5. "Sakuntala and the Ring of Remembrance" completed as a lecture-text in the summer of 1993; his last critical piece.

SECONDARY SOURCES

Rao, M.R. 1965. "Review of *Fifteen Poems from a Classical Tamil Anthology*." *Literary Criterion* : 6 : 4 : 108-09.

Raffel, Burton. 1966. "Review of *The Striders* by A.K. Ramanujan." *Mahfil* (now *Journal of South Asian Literature*) : 3 : 2-3 : 85-88.

Bains, Y.S. 1967. "Review of *The Striders* by A.K. Ramanujan." *Literature East and West* : 11 : 1 : Mar. : 72.

Zinnes, Harriet. 1967. "A Review of *The Striders* by A.K. Ramanujan." *Prairie Schooner* : 41 : 3 : 353.

Ireland, K. 1967. "Three Poets." *Journal of Commonwealth Literature* : 4 : Dec. : 139-42. [contains review of *The Striders*.]

Vaish, Y.N. 1969. "A.K. Ramanujan : Escapist." *Thought* : 21 : 25 : 21 Jun. : 14-15.

Nakulan. 1969. "A Meeting with A.K. Ramanujan." *Thought* : 21 : Nov. : 11-13.

Lal, P. 1969. "Precise and Passionate Sincerities." *The Alien Insider*. Calcutta : Writers Workshop, 1987, 106-08. (Review of *The Striders*.)

Singh, Satyanarain. 1969. "Ramanujan and Ezekiel." *Osmania Journal of English Studies* : 7 : 1 : 67-75. Also in 1971. *The Miscellany* : 45 : 47-56 and in 1980. Kulshrestha, Chiranthan. Ed. *Contemporary Indian English Verse : An Evaluation*. New Delhi : Arnold-Heinemann : 165-74.

Aon, 1970. "Review of Hokkulalli Hoovila by A.K. Ramanujan." *The Illustrated Weekly of India* : 91 : 39 : 27 Sep. : 47.

Ezekiel, Nissim. 1972. "Two Poets : A.K. Ramanujan and Keki N. Daruwalla." *The Illustrated Weekly of India* : 93 : 25 : 18 Jun. : 43-45. Also in his 1992. *Selected Prose*. Delhi : Oxford : 147-53. (Review of *Relations*)

Gowda, H.H. Anniah. 1973. "Indian Plays and Poems in English : Karnad's *Tughlaq* and Ramanujan's *Relations*." *Literary Half-Yearly* : 14 : 1 : Jan. : 3-10.

Nagarajan, S. 1975. "A.K. Ramanujan." in Vinson, James and Kirkpatrick, D.L. Eds. *Contemporary Poets*. London : St. James Press : 1230-32.

Parthasarathy, R. 1976. "How It Strikes a Contemporary : The Poetry of A.K. Ramanujan." *Literary Criterion* : 12 : 2-3 : 187-97. Also in 1977. *Osmania Journal of English Studies* : 13 : 187-99.

Upadhyay, M.N. 1976. "A.K. Ramanujan." *The Illustrated Weekly of India* : 97 : 29 : 08 Jul. : 21-23. [An interview repudiated by the poet.]

Anon, 1977. "Review of *Selected Poems* by A.K. Ramanujan." *Indian Book Chronicle* : 7 : 11 : 1 Apr.

Bhabha, Homi. 1978. "Indo-Anglian Attitudes." *Times Literary Supplement* : 3 Feb. : 136. (Contains review of *Selected Poems*.)

Nathan, Leonard. 1978. "Plain Speech for a God : *Speaking of Siva* by A.K. Ramanujan." *Journal of South Asian Literature* : 13.

Nabar, Vrinda. 1978. "Review of *Selected Poems* by A.K.

Ramanujan." *World Literature Written in English* : 17 : 2 : Nov. : 545-47.

Guptara, Prabhu S. 1978. "Review of *Selected Poems* by A.K. Ramanujan." *Modern Literature Today* : 52 : 2 : Spring : 344.

Chakrabarti, Ashis. 1979. "Review of A.K. Ramanujan's *Selected Poems*." *The Statesman* : 30 Dec. : III : 1.

Kulshrestha, Chirantan. 1979. "The Self in A.K. Ramanujan's Poetry." *Indian Journal of English Studies* : 18 : 108-19. Also in his 1980. Ed. *Contemporary Indian English Verse : An Evaluation*. New Delhi : Arnold Heinemann : 175-86 and in 1981. *World Literature Written in English* : 20 : 1 : Spring : 162-72.

Mishra, Rabi S. 1979. "A.K. Ramanujan : A Point of View." *Chandrabhaga* : 1 : 60-66.

Guptara, Prabhu. 1979. "The Individual and the Community in the Poetry of A.K. Ramanujan." In Massa, Daniel. Ed. *Individual and Community in Commonwealth Literature*. Msida : Univ. of Malta Press : 177-87.

Rao, K. Raghavendra. 1979. "Reverse Romanticism : The Case of A.K. Ramanujan's *The Striders*." In Naik, M.K. Ed. *Aspects of Indian Writing in English*. Delhi : Macmillan : 120-25.

Jha, Rama. 1980. "Between Two Worlds." *Times of India* (Sunday) : 20 Jan. : III.

Priadevi. 1980. "Review of *Interior Landscape* by A.K. Ramanujan." *Youth Times* : 1 Feb. : 54-55.

Mirza, Taqi Ali. 1980. "A.K. Ramanujan's 'Particular Hell.'" In Shahane, V.A. and Sivaramakrishna, M. Eds. *Indian Poetry in English : A Critical Assessment*. Delhi : Macmillan : 152-61.

Sundari, G. and K.S. Ramamurti. 1981. "Robert Lowell's 'My Last Afternoon with Uncle Deveurux Winslow' and A.K. Ramanujan's 'Small-Scale Reflections on a Great House' : A Study in Comparison." *Indian Scholar* : 3 : 1 : Jan. : 75-84.

Jha, Rama. 1981. "A Conversation with A.K. Ramanujan." *Humanities Review* : 3 : 1 : 1981 : 5-13. [An important interview.]

Devy, G.N. 1981. "Alienation as Means of Self-Exploration : A Study of A.K. Ramanujan's Poetry." *Chandrabhaga* : 6 : Winter : 5-19.

Dwivedi, A.N. 1981. "Theme and Form in Ramanujan's Poetry." *Rajasthan Journal of English Studies* : 13-14 : 150-60.

Pal, K.S. 1981. *Nissim Ezekiel and A.K. Ramanujan : A Comparative Study*. Gorgoti : Asha Prakashan.

Amanuddin, Syed. 1981. "Moraes and Ramanujan." *World Poetry in English*. New Delhi : Sterling : 119-26.

Sreenivasan, S. 1982. "Irony in A.K. Ramanujan's Poetry : A Note." *Journal of Literature and Aesthetics* : 2 : 4 : Oct. : 109-16.

Dwivedi, A.N. 1982. "The Poetry of A.K. Ramanujan : Cultural Ambivalence and Personal Dilemma." *Journal of South Asian Literature* : 17 : 1 : Winter-Spring : 241-48.

Anon, 1983. "Review of *Hymns for Drowning*." *Times of India* : 20 Mar. : 8 : 1-5.

Banerjee, Purabi. 1983. "A Seasoned Poet Speaks." *The Hindustan Times* (Mag) : 17 Apr. : IV : 5-8.

Dasgupta, Chidanand, 1983. "Suddenly a Phrase Begins to Sing." *Span* : Nov : 32-34.

Dwivedi, A.N. 1983. *A.K. Ramanujan and His Poetry*. Delhi : Doaba House.

Lall, Emmanuel N. 1983. "A.K. Ramanujan." *The Poetry of Encounter*. New Delhi : Sterling : 42-64.

Mohanty, Niranjan. 1983. "The Home-Bound Pilgrim : A Study of A.K. Ramanujan's Poetry." *Indian Journal of English Studies* : 22 : 39-48.

Dwivedi, A.N. 1984. "A.K. Ramanujan as a Poet of Love." *Journal of Indian Writing in English* : 12 : 1 : Jan. : 1-6.

Chellappan, K. and K. Bhashyam. 1984. "Encounter and Synthesis in the Poetry of A.K. Ramanujan." *Journal of Indian Writing in English* : 12 : 2 : Jul. : 96-104.

Parameswaran, R. and Uma Parameswaran. 1984. "Singing to The Feet of the Lord : On A.K. Ramanujan's Translations from Nammalvar's Poetry." *Journal of South Asian Literature* : 19 : 2.

Naik, M.K. 1984. "A.K. Ramanujan and the Search for Roots." *Dimensions of Indian English Literature*. New Delhi : Sterling : 14-24. Also in 1989. Prasad, Madhusudan. Ed. *Living Indian English Poets*. New Delhi : Sterling : 13-23.

Srinath, C.N. 1984. "The Poetry of A.K. Ramanujan." In Dwivedi, A.N. Ed. *Contemporary Indo-English Verse*, Vol. 2. Bareilly : Prakash : 29-34.

Desai, S.K. 1984. "Mixing Memory and Desire." In Naik, M.K. Ed. *Perspectives on Indian Poetry in English*. Delhi : Abhinav : 109-23.

Mukherjee, Swapan K. 1985. "Theme and Form of Ramanujan's Poetry." *Patriot* : 30 Jan. : 4 : 3-7.

Das, Bijay Kumar. 1985. "Ramanujan's 'A River' : An Explication." *Journal of Indian Writing in English* : 13 : 2.

Anon, 1986. "Review of *Poems of Love and War*." *Tribune* (Mag) : 6 Jun. : II : 3-5.

Jagdes, Prafulla K. 1986. "Murugan and Kali Mocked : The Religious Poems of Ramanujan and Shiv K. Kumar." *Journal of Literary Studies* : 9 : 1-2 : Jun.-Dec. : 27-50.

Anon, 1986. "Review of *Poems of Love and War*." *Indian Express* (Mag) : 17 Aug. : 5 : 4-8.

Anon, 1986. "Review of *Second Sight*." *Indian Express* (Mag) : 9 Nov. : V : 1-2.

Naik, M.K. 1986. "Landscapes and Inscapes : Review of *Second Sight*." *Kavya Bharati* : 1 : 65-71.

Anon, 1986. "Review of *Poems of Love and War*." *Literary Criterion* : 21 : 1-2 : 121-23.

Anon, 1987. "Review of *Second Sight*." *Indian Literature* : 30 : 1 : Jan.-Feb. : 121-24.

Anon, 1987. "Review of *Second Sight.*" *Indian PEN* : 48 : 1 : Jan.-Mar. : 20-21.

Anon, 1988. "Review of *Poems of Love and War.*" *Indian Literature* : 31 : 2 : Mar.-Apr. : 143-47.

John, Joseph. 1988. "A.K. Ramanujan : *Second Sight.*" *Journal of South Asian Literature* : 23.

Srivastava, Ramesh K. 1989. "Reflection of Growing Dehumanisation in Ramanujan's Poetry." In Ram Atma ed. *Contemporary Indian English Poetry*. Calcutta : Writers Workshop : 51-63.

Reuben, Elizabeth. 1989. "The Presence of the Past : The Sense of Time in the Poetry of A.K. Ramanujan." *Journal of Indian Writing in English* : 17 : 1 : Jan. : 13-20.

Matilal, Bimal Krishna. 1989. "*Confrontations of Culture.* Calcutta : K.P. Bagchi & Co.

Talwar, Shashi. 1989. "A.K. Ramanujan's Image of India." In Dhawan, R.K. *et al.* Eds. *Recent Commonwealth Literature.* New Delhi : Prestige : 74-80.

Dulai, S.S. 1989. "First and Only Sight." *Journal of South Asian Literature* : 24 : 2 : 149-75.

Raghunandan, Lakshmi. 1990. "A.K. Ramanujan." *Contemporary Indian Poetry in English*. New Delhi : Reliance : 150-202.

Kurup, P.K.J. 1991. "The Self in the Poetry of A.K. Ramanujan." *Contemporary Indian Poetry in English*. New Delhi : Atlantic : 180-241.

King, Bruce. 1991. "A.K. Ramanujan." *Three Indian Poets.* Madras : Oxford : 60-103.

Choudhury, Indra Nath. 1992. "A.K. Ramanujan : The Context-Sensity [Sic] Man." *Indian Horizon* : 41 : 4 : 81-86.

Wasi, Muriel. 1992. "Remembering Poet, Scholar, A.K. Ramanujan." *Indian Horizon* : 41 : 4 : 87-90.

Kalven, Jamie. 1992. "Catching India by the Tale." *The University of Chicago Magazine*. Also in 1993. *Span* : Jun. : 44-45.

Sengupta, S. 1992. "Quest for Identity or Reappraisal? A Second Look at Ramanujan's Poetry." *Creative Forum* : 5 :

1-4 : Jan.-Dec. : 82-94. Also in Pathak, R.S. Ed. *Quest for Identity in Indian English Writing*, Vol. 2. New Delhi : Bahri : 82-94.

Susanne & Lloyd Rudolph. 1993. "Remembering Raman." *The Times of India*, 25 July, p. 8.

Anon, 1993. "Author Dead." *The Statesman* 16 July.

Anon, 1993. "Ramanujan Dead." *The Indian Express* 16 July.

Mohanty, Niranjan. 1993. "Things as They Are : The Poetry of A.K. Ramanujan." *Journal of South Asian Literature* : 28 : 1&2 : Spring-Fall : 167-80. Also in 1998. Bhatnagar, M.K. Ed. *Indian Writings in English*, Vol. 1. New Delhi : Atlantic : 60-72.

Karim, N.A. 1993. "A.K. Ramanujan." *Mainstream* : 31 : 38 31 Jul. : 5-6.

Ezekiel, Nissim. 1993. "Small-Scale Reflections on a Great Friend." *The Deccan Herald* : 24 Jul. : 4.

Anon, 1993. "A.K. Ramanujan." *The Book Review* : 17 : 8 : Aug. : 4-5.

Dwivedi, A.N. 1993. "The Passing Away of a Poet." *Northern India Patrika* (Allahabad) : 17 Aug. : 7.

Sharma, R.C. *et al.* 1993. "Ramanujan's Legacy." *Indian Review of Books* : 11 : Aug.-Sep. : 27-34.

Anon, 1993. "Review of *Folktales from India*." *Economic Times* : 24 Oct. : 13 : 2-8.

Anon, 1993. "Review of *Folktales from India*." *The Book Review* : 17 : 12 : Dec. : 4.

Pandey, M.S. 1993. "Indianness in A.K. Ramanujan's Poetry." *Language Forum* 19 : 1&2 : 112-19. Also in 1994. Pathak, R.S. Ed. *Indianization of English Language and Literature*. New Delhi : Bahri : 112-19.

Reddy, K. Venkata. 1994. "Poetry of Encounter and Synthesis : A Look at A.K. Ramanujan." *Journal of Indian Writing in English* : 22 : 1 : Jan. : 13-17.

Trikha, Pradeep. 1994. "A.K. Ramanujan's Fascinating Tapestry." *Literary Criterion* : 19 : 2.

Dharwadker, Vinay. 1994. "Post-Colonial Cosmopolitanism : A Note on A.K. Ramanujan's Theory and Practice of

Criticism and Translation." *Indian Literature* : 160 : Mar.-Apr. : 91-97.

Ananthamurthy, U.R. 1994. "The Gentle Genius." *Littcrit* : 21 : 1 : Jun. : 5-8.

Paniker, K. Ayyappa. 1994. "A.K. Ramanujan : A Restless Soul." *Littcrit* : 20 : 1 : Jun. : 9-12.

Ananathamurthy, U.R. 1994. "A.K. Ramanujan : A Connoisseur of the Arts of Life and Poetry." *Indian Literature* : 162 : Jul.-Aug. : 9-12.

Sharada Prasad, H.Y. 1994. "A.K. Ramanujan : A Tribute." *Indian Literature* : 162 : Jul.-Aug. : 13-16.

Daruwalla, K.N. 1994. "Ramanujan : The Expatriate Local." *Indian Literature* : 162 : Jul.-Aug. : 17-25.

Das, Bijay Kumar. 1994. "Ramanujan, the Poet : An Overview." *Indian Literature* : 162 : Jul.-Aug. : 26-31.

Mohanty, Niranjan. 1994. "Chicago and AKR." *Indian Literature* : 162 : Jul.-Aug. : 32-42.

Dwivedi, A.N. 1994. "*Second Sight* : Indianness of A.K. Ramanujan's Poetry." *Indian Literature* : 162 : Jul.-Aug. : 43-59.

Dallmayr, Fred. 1994. "Western Thought and Indian Thought : Comments on Ramanujan." *Philosophy East and West* : 44 : 3 : Jul. : 527-42.

Anon, 1994. "Review of *The Interior Landscape*." *The Book Review* : 18 : 10 : Oct. :15.

Dharwadker, Vinay. 1994. "A.K. Ramanujan : Author, Translator, Scholar." *World Literature Today* : 68 : 2 : 279-80.

Sharma, N.L. 1994. "Impact of American Milieu and Quest for Reality in A.K. Ramanujan's Poetry." In Bala, Suman. Ed. *American Literature Today*. New Delhi : Prestige : 181-88.

Reddy, K. Venkata. 1994. "Recollection Emotionalized in Untranquil Moments." *Critical Studies in Commonwealth Literature*. New Delhi : Prestige : 88-93.

Karnad, Girish. 1995. "Poems of Pain." *Indian Express* : 3 Aug. : 4.

Parameswaran, P. 1995. "A.K. Ramanujan as Translator of

Cankam Classics : An Assessment." *Journal of Institute of Asian Studies* : 12 : 2 : Mar. : 49-110.

Moraes, Dom. 1995. "Raman's Way." *The Times of India* (Sunday) : 18 Jun. : 2.

Daruwalla, K.N. 1995. "Forging Contraries : Review of *Collected Poems*." *The Book Review* : 19 : 8 : Aug. : 33-34.

Ezekiel, Nissim. 1995. "Review of *Collected Poems*." *India Today*.

Naqui, Roomy. 1995. "The Language of Silence : An Analysis of A.K. Ramanujan's 'On the Death of a Poem.'" *Revaluations* : 1 : 3 : 75-79.

Dwivedi, A.N. 1995. *The Poetic Art of A.K. Ramanujan*. New Delhi : B.R. Publishers : 1-168.

Das, B.K. 1995. "The Importance of Being A.K. Ramanujan." *Aspects of Commonwealth Literature*. New Delhi : Creative : 40-48.

Patke, Rajeev S. 1995. "Ithacan Voyages : The Poetry of R. Parthasarathy and A.K. Ramanujan." In Yaravinteliamath, C.R. *et al.* Eds. *New Perspectives in Indian Literature in English*. New Delhi : Sterling : 112-26.

Nair, Rama. 1995. "A.K. Ramanujan : A Study in Psychological Realism." In Dhawan, R.K. Ed. *Indian Literature Today*, Vol. 2. New Delhi : Prestige : 32-39.

Talwar, Shashi Bala. 1995. "Imagery in Ramanujan's Poetry." In Dhawan, R.K. Ed. *Indian Literature Today*. Vol. 2 : 40-48.

Bhatt, Sujata. 1996. "Connect and then Disconnect." *Poetry Review* : 86 : 1 : Spring : 70-72.

Rao, P.M. 1996. "The Poetry of Exile." In Bhatnagar, M.K. Ed. *Indian Writings in English*, Vol. 1. New Delhi : Atlantic : 59-67.

Chindhade, Shirish. 1996. "A.K. Ramanujan." *Five Indian English Poets*. New Delhi : Atlantic : 62-90.

Sumana, K. 1996. "A Realist Look at Ramanujan's 'A River.'" In Rao, C.R. Visveswara. Ed. *Indian Writing Today* : Delhi : Indian Association for English Studies : 39-41.

Jayaprada, C.L.L. 1996. "A Stylistic Approach to Ramanujan's

'Still Another View of Grace.'" In Rao, C.R. Visweswara. Ed. *Indian Literature Today* : 42-47.

Naqui, Roomy. 1996. "A Poetics of Space." *Indian Literature* : 39 : 3 : May-Jun. : 145-146.

Pandey, Mithilesh K. 1997. "The Cult of Culture and Ethos : A.K. Ramanujan's *Relations*." *Veer Kunwar Singh University Journal of English Studies* : 3 : 15-21.

Rao, D. Venkata. 1997. "The Ruptured Idiom : of Dellmayr, Matilal and Ramanujan's Way of Thinking." *Journal of Indian Council of Philosophical Research* : 14 : 2 : Jan.-Apr. : 99-121.

Rao, K.R. 1997. "A.K. Ramanujan and the Poetics of Order." *The Literary Half-Yearly* : 38 : 2 : Jul. : 102-06.

Chellappan, K. 1997. "A.K. Ramanujan : The Translator-Creator." *Kavya Bharati* : 9 : 208-23.

Pandey, Maya Shanker 1997. "Animal Imagery in the Poetry of A.K. Ramanujan." *Aligarh Journal of English Studies* : 19 : 1 : 73-83.

Kumar, Akshay. 1998. "Parody as Subterfuge : Cultural Politics of A.K. Ramanujan Poetry." *New Quest* : 127 : Jan.-Feb. : 10.

Ramazani, Jahan. 1998. "Metaphor and Postcoloniality : The Poetry of A.K. Ramanujan." *Contemporary Literature* : 39 : 1 : Spring : 27-53.

Pandey, Surya Nath. 1998. "Feminist Concerns in Ramanujan's Poetry." *Studies in Contemporary Poets* : New Delhi : Atlantic : 91-101. Also in *Journal of Indian Writing in English* : 26 : 2 : Jul. : 14-25.

Balachandran, Ponni. 1999. "Man and Destiny in the Poems of A.K. Ramanujan." In Pandey, Mithilesh K. Ed. *Contemporary Indian Literature in English : A Humanistic Perspective*. Ludhiana : Kalyani : 23-29.

Saha, Subhas C. 1999. "The Indian Cultural Perspective in A.K. Ramanujan's Poetry." In Pandey, Mithilesh K. Ed. *Recent Indian Literature in English*. New Delhi : Anmol Publishers : 19-26.

Singer, Milton B., Edward C. Dimock, Jr. and Krishna Ramanujan. 1999. "Two Tributes to A.K. Ramanujan" in Dharwadker, Vinay. Ed. *The Collected Essays of A.K. Ramanujan*. New Delhi : Oxford : xii-xviii.

Kumar, Akshaya. 1999. "Contempt Disguised as Concern : Orientalist Reconstruction of Home/Nation in the Poetry of A.K. Ramanujan and R. Parthasarathy." *Kavya Bharati*. 11 : 197-206.

Notes on Contributors

D. Ramakrishna is an authority on Edgar Allan Poe and visited University of Texas at Austin as a Fulbright Post-Doctoral Fellow in 1992. Armed with about half-a-dozen critical volumes, he is currently working on his forthcoming *The Craft of Poe's Tales*. Dr. Ramakrishna is Professor of English at Kakatiya University, Warangal.

Surya Nath Pandey has extensively worked in the area of contemporary Literature. His publications include *Stephen Spender : A Study in Poetic Growth* (New Jersey : Humanities Press, 1982, and *Studies in Contemporary Poets* (New Delhi : Atlantic, 1998) besides edited volumes on Movement Poets, Postcoloniality, Nissim Ezekiel and Feminist Writing. Dr. Pandey is a Senior Professor of English at Banaras Hindu University, Varanasi.

Niranjan Mohanty is a distinguished critic and poet with five verse-volumes in English to his credit including *Prayers to Lord Jagannath*. An extensively published scholar, he participated in the International Writing Programme, University of Iowa in 1994. Dr. Mohanty is professor of English at the University of Viswa-Bharati, Santiniketan.

Rajalakshmi Gopalan holds a Doctorate from the University of Madras. She has published several essays in periodicals and anthologies. She is presently working on a project on Canadian Women novelists. Dr. Gopalan is Lecturer in English at Qaid-e-Millat Govt. College, Madras.

Rakesh N. Desai has a doctoral dissertation on W.H. Auden's poetry. He has presented papers in various seminars on Indian English and American poetry. Dr. Desai is Reader in English at South Gujarat University, Surat.

Mohan Ramanan is a perceptive critic and scholar well-known for his book on Movement Poets and also for his seminal contributions to American Literature. Dr. Ramanan is Professor of English at the University of Hyderabad.

Bijay Kumar Das is a noted critic with publications like *Aspects of Commonwealth Literature, Twentieth Century English Criticism* and *Horizon of Translation Studies* among others. Dr. Das is Reader in English at Ravenshaw College, Cuttack.

E.V. Ramakrishnan writes both in English and Malayalam. His recent publications in English include *A Python in a Snake Park* and *Making It New*. Dr. Ramakrishnan is Reader in English at South Gujarat University, Surat.

Jayaprakash A. Shinde has published papers on Third World Literature and Modern British Literature in several journals and anthologies. He is presently conducting a UGC project in English Language Development. Dr. Shinde is Reader in English at Shivaji University, Kolhapur.

Premila Paul has published articles and books on Indian Literature and Feminist Aesthetics both in India and abroad. She is Reader in English at American College, Madurai.

Shirish V. Chindhade has written on several Indian and British writers besides bringing out a discerning volume *Five Indian English Poets*. Dr. Chindhade is Principal at M.U. College, Pimpri, Pune.

P.K. Kalyani has worked in the areas of Indian writing in English and Contemporary Literature. She is Lecturer in English at M.S. University, Tirunelveli.

Rama Nair has many prestigious publications to her credit including *Indian Theories of Language : A Literary Approach* and *The Poetry and Translations of A.K. Ramanujan* (Forthcoming). Dr. Nair is Reader in English at Osmania University, Hyderabad.

Rita Kothari has published essays in the areas of Post-Coloniality and Translation. Her forthcoming volume *Modern Gujarati Poetry in English Translation* is to be published by Sahitya Akademi. Ms. Kothari is Lecturer in English at St. Xavier's College, Ahmedabad.